HX 84. D5 C65 1990

Daniel De Leon

LIVES of the LEFT is a new series of original biographies of leading figures in the European and North American socialist and labour movements. Short, lively and accessible, they will be welcomed by students of history and politics and by anyone interested in the development of the Left. *general editor* David Howell

published: **J. Ramsay MacDonald** Austen Morgan
James Maxton William Knox
Karl Kautsky Dick Geary
'Big Bill' Haywood Melvyn Dubofsky
A. J. Cook Paul Davies
R. H. Tawney Anthony Wright
Thomas Johnston Graham Walker
Arthur Henderson Fred Leventhal
William Lovett Joel Wiener

forthcoming, to include: **John Strachey** Mike Newman
Aneurin Bevan Dai Smith
Ernest Bevin Peter Weiler
Eugene Debs Gail Malmgreen
John Reed Eric Homberger
J. A. Hobson Jules Townsend
George Orwell Stephen Ingle

LIVES of the LEFT

Daniel De Leon

Stephen Coleman

Manchester University Press

Manchester and New York

Distributed exclusively in the USA and Canada by St. Martin's Press, New York

Copyright © Stephen Coleman 1990

Published by Manchester University Press,
Oxford Road, Manchester, M13 9PL, UK
and Room 400, 175 Fifth Avenue, New York, NY 10010, USA

Distributed exclusively in the USA and Canada
by St. Martin's Press, Inc., 175 Fifth Avenue, New York, NY 10010, USA

British Library cataloguing in publication data
  Coleman, Stephen
  Daniel De Leon. — (Lives of the left)
  1. United States. Socialism. De Leon, Daniel, 1852–1914
  I. Title   II. Series
  335'.00973

Library of Congress cataloging in publication data
Coleman, Stephen. 1956–
  Daniel De Leon / Stephen Coleman.
      p.   cm. — (Lives of the left)
  ISBN 0-7190-2190-1
  1. De Leon, Daniel, 1852-1914. 2. Socialists—United States—Biography.
  I. Title.   II. Series.
  HX84.D5C65 1989
  335'.0092—dc29   89-12713

ISBN 0 7190 2190 1 *hardback*

Set in Perpetua
by Koinonia Ltd, Manchester

Printed in Great Britain
by Robert Hartnoll Ltd, Bodmin, Cornwall

Contents

Preface

This biography is a study of uncompromised revolutionary hope and dismal political failure. The story of Daniel De Leon is not that of a populist leader or a radical legislator, but of a militant and unswerving Marxist and irrepressible socialist activist who could see what was wrong and what must be changed in the mean and sordid atmosphere of turn-of-the-century American capitalism. The wrongs which he exposed and the change which he sought concerned not only the nature of the capitalist system itself, but also the ways in which that system tends to dominate and misdirect efforts to resist it. The wrongs were to outlive De Leon; the change has yet to come. Still people of reason argue with passion, and sometimes despair, about why socialist ideas have never taken root in the USA; why the American working class has been so successfully accommodated within the capitalist system; why the message of De Leon has been so utterly unheeded. It is to be hoped that this biographical study of the pioneer of American Marxism will contribute to an explanation of the hopes and failures which characterised the early socialist tradition in the USA.

Writers of history have not been kind to Daniel De Leon. Apart from the generally uncritical hagiographical accounts of his life written by De Leonists in defence of their tradition, most historians have mentioned De Leon only in passing, usually disparagingly and often inaccurately. When I first came to study the history of socialist thought in the USA, I was surprised (and irritated) to discover that no serious scholarly work dealing exclusively with De Leon's ideas had been published. It reminded me of the absence of serious scholarly works on the great English Marxist, William Morris, which had at one time been a feature of British socialist historiography. It was clear to me from the outset that De Leon was a figure of major intellectual importance in the history of American socialist thought, and it was just not good enough for his life and ideas to be left to the realm of superficial caricature. As I embarked upon a study of De Leon's writings and speeches it became obvious that I was considering a substantial political theorist, an evaluation of whom should not be clouded by tedious psychological investigations or other long-obsolete sectarian squabbles. In the time that I have written this book I have come to conclude that most of the original attacks upon De Leon were motivated by the fact that he would not abandon his principles in order to court the kind of popularity socialist often attract when they stop being socialists. The secondary critics of De Leon have too often been inclined simply to regurgitate the prejudices of those who wrote before them without comprehending the political context of such prejudices. I must plead guilty to an absence of biographical interest in the deeper qualities or defects of De Leon's personality, nor would I expect others to evaluate the political ideas of a Marx, a Mill or a Morris on the basis of criteria which are best left to computer dating agencies. In so far as De Leon's character influenced his effect as a political thinker and activist such matters are considered in the following pages. It is my hope that readers will be motivated by this account of De Leon's life to turn next to his many very readable and easily available writings, in which are to be found some of the soundest and most straightforward Marxist thinking between the years 1890 and 1914. The account which follows is intended to clarify the context and meaning of such writings, as well as to raise a number of criticisms which the open-minded reader will want to consider.

I acknowledge with gratitude the contributions to the production of this book of several people. Melvin Harris, whose profound intellectual generosity has been an inspiration to me, allowed me free access to his unique collection of material by and on De Leon; furthermore, the discussions I had with him and the suggestions I received helped me immensely to understand some of the important themes examined in this book. Frank Girard entertained me while I was researching in the USA, offered me the benefit of his years of scholarly and committed reflection upon De Leon's contribution to the socialist movement, and (together with Ben Perry, with whom he is writing what promises to be an excellent history of the Socialist Labor Party) gave me insights into the De

Leonist tradition which I could not have obtained otherwise. Adam Buick has encouraged and, sometimes, directed my research, especially into De Leon's conception of socialism. Clifford Slapper's very useful comments on the text and consistently intelligent suggestions of ways to improve both the stylistic and political quality of this book are much appreciated. I have received useful information from Edmund Grant, Ronald A. Sims, John O'Neil, Louis Lazarus and a number of others in the USA who did not know me personally but who heard that I was writing about De Leon and were kind enough to send me literature by, or about, him. In expressing my sincere thanks to these people, I must make clear that I take responsibility for any errors of fact or fault of interpretation which may have found their way into the text. I would also like to thank Sally McCann for her diligent and very helpful work in copy-editing this book. Above all, I dedicate this book to my father, who first taught me about the importance of history and the vision of socialism, which, when combined, can change the world; without his support over many years this book could never have been written.

Stephen Coleman

1 The enigma of Daniel De Leon

Socialists whose lofty aim is to create a society of fraternal co-operation and communal harmony have spent much of their history heaping abuse upon one another in an often acrimonious debate about the best way to reach the promised land of socialism. Militant socialists who have refused to compromise their principles in accordance with what their opponents declare to be the pragmatic requirements of living with capitalism have been derided by so-called 'practical socialists' or 'possibilists' as intransigent dogmatists, or 'impossibilists'. The non-compromisers have, in turn, questioned the socialist credentials of the possibilist 'trimmers', suggesting that such people are betraying the socialist goal by becoming sucked in to the political immediacies of running capitalism. Defenders of the capitalist system, to whom the subjugation of the pursuit of profit for the pursuit of principle is almost incomprehensible, must have been frequently bewildered and delighted to see the socialist foe so intensely engaged in campaigns to discredit one another, so bitterly perpetuating their own disunity in a relentless fight about who properly belongs with the socialist camp.

Daniel De Leon was the most outstanding American socialist thinker, writer, orator and political organiser of the years from 1890 until the eve of the First World War. He joined the Socialist Labor Party in 1890 and was to be the dominate influence upon it for twenty-four years: as editor of its newspaper, nationwide public speaker and most eminent theoreti-

1

cian. On several occasions, he stood for public office as a socialist candidate. For fifteen years he campaigned relentlessly to win over the unions to support for socialism. When this failed, he was active in forming a revolutionary union movement to rival the 'pure and simple' capitalist unions, and in 1905 he was an enthusiastic co-founder of the Industrial Workers of the World (IWW). He attended congresses of the Second International, repeatedly denouncing the non-revolutionary nature of the movement and elaborating a coherent criticism of the strategy of 'socialist reformism'. De Leon was an uncompromising social revolutionary: a man who sought to end, not merely amend, the profit system. As such, he was fiercely detested and reviled, not only by capitalism's apologists but also by those reformers who regarded him as the ultimately inflexible Marxist idealogue. The abuse did not flow in one direction only: De Leon's acidic hostility towards all who adulterated socialist principles created numerous enemies for him on the Left. He called them 'labor fakers' and 'labor lieutenants of capital', and regarded the toothless reformists on the Left as greater obstacles to working-class emancipation than the avowed defenders of capitalism.

To catalogue the expressions of antagonism towards De Leon by his contemporaries on the Left is to demonstrate unequivocally that this is not a biography of a man who was everybody's friend. Samuel Gompers, the President of the American Federation of Labor (AFL) and the most frequent victim of De Leon's charge of being a 'faker', wrote despairingly that 'This man's characteristics of intolerance to everyone that does not adopt his policy, his venom and spite crop out at every opportunity [and] that makes it impossible for anyone that has any self respect to have any dealings with him or those for whom he speaks.[1] Such was Gomper's dislike of De Leon that he had to be censured by William Cunnane of the New

Bedford Strike Committee in 1898 for telling the strikers that De Leon was a Pinkerton agent, that is, a paid union-smasher. 'Big' Bill Haywood described De Leon as 'the theorizing professor' whose 'only contact with the workers was through the ideas with which he wished to "indoctrinate" them'.[2] John O'Neill, the 'moderate' editor of the *Miners' Magazine*, referred to De Leon's supporters as 'a bunch of tramps' who 'became infuriated at every laboring man that did not recognise De Leon as the triple-crowned pope of the labor movement'[3] Such references to De Leon as a 'pope' were common, while O'Neill added anti-Semitic abuse of De Leon to his attack for good measure. The Eton-educated English 'Marxist', H. M. Hyndman, wrote in his journal, *Justice*, that 'De Leon, who was a man of ability, and did good work in his time . . . has carefully destroyed his own party and driven away all the best men.'[4] On other occasions, *Justice* stooped to racist abuse against De Leon, in accordance with Hyndman's own anti-Semitic prejudice. For example, when Hyndman's Social Democratic Federation (SDF) expelled the Scottish 'impossibilists' who adhered to De Leon's ideas, *Justice* commented that 'the prompt action of the SDF in dealing with those malcontents who are bent upon following the German-Venezuelan Jew Loeb or De Leon to the pit of infamy and disgrace, is regarded with some satisfaction on this side.'[5] 'In resigning from De Leon's Socialist Labor Party (SLP), Charles H. Matchett, who had stood as its Vice-Presidential candidate in 1892 and Presidential candidate in 1896, wrote that 'I have completely lost all confidence and trust in De Leon . . . his was the power to unify, to harmonize but he has disrupted the party.'[6] James Connolly started out as a comrade and admirer of De Leon, but was certainly not so by 1908, when he described him as a 'scoundrel' and 'egregious egotist', as well as a dogmatist and sectarian.[7]

3

The fiercest blows were provided by De Leon's gradualist, reformist opponents in the Socialist Party of America (SPA) who could not tolerate his uncompromising revolutionary stance. At the SPA's 1908 Convention, Ben Hanford, the party's Vice-Presidential candidate, declared that '. . . I want nothing to do with Bill Sykes, the burglar; I want nothing to do and no communication with Jesse James, the train robber; I want nothing to do with Daniel De Leon, the union wrecker . . .'[8]

Another leading figure of the SPA, the lawyer, Morris Hillquit, described De Leon as ' . . . a fanatic. A keen thinker and merciless logician, he was carried away beyond the realm of reality by the process of his own abstract and somewhat Talmudistic logic.'[9] Perhaps the most bitter assault upon De Leon by his SPA opponents occurred when he died. On 13 May 1914 the following harsh judgement appeared in the *New Yorker Volkszeitung*, the newspaper of those 'socialists' who De Leon spared no energy in depicting as enemies of the working-class interest:

> He, who expired on Monday evening, fared as did so many before him, he died a few decades too late; he outlived himself.
>
> True to his maxim to destroy what he could not rule, he concentrated, during the last fifteen years, his vitality and will-power upon tearing down what he, personally, had helped to create.
>
> And therein he was great, far greater than in construction and erection. De Leon was, indeed, a destructive genius, i.e. he was great in demolishing, in tearing down. With an hatred that was insatiable and unstillable, he fought since his entrance into the American labor movement . . . against every movement of the working class of this country that showed success and that seemed to be in the ascendancy.

The obituary continues for several more paragraphs, each crammed with heartfelt hatred towards the almost demonic De Leon. It is odd to think that only four years earlier the author of such comments had sat as fellow delegate with De Leon at the Copenhagen Congress of the Second International, yet by 1914 had far more literary bullets to fire at a dead 'comrade' than at the open defenders of capitalist interests.

The legacy of the contemporary vilification of De Leon has been its repetition by historians and other writers in the years since 1914. Mervyn Dubofsky, in his history of the IWW, says of De Leon that 'Desiring to be an American Lenin, he compelled uniformity among his disciples. He shared Lenin's iron will as well as his intense desire to command men and to make history.'[10] A recent biographer of Debs refers to De Leon's 'arbitrary manner and ruthless condemnation of any who disagreed with him . . .'.[11] Holbrook wrote that De Leon was 'a man who had no peer as a doctrinaire. No theologian made finer distinction in matters of dogma than De Leon could muster in socialism.'[12] The same caricature was trotted out by Chewter, in his account of De Leon's influence in Britain: 'His was a very powerful personality, capable of attracting tremendous admiration and affection from those of his followers who were willing to accept his word as gospel. But let anyone challenge his authority, or his ideological reasoning, and his intolerance and hostility knew no bounds.'[13] Barbara Tuchman tells her readers that De Leon was a 'fanatic dictator' and that he 'was convinced that only he was fitted to lead the class struggle'.[14] Raymond Challinor, also writing on De Leon's British impact, comments that De Leon's works were 'sometimes marred by sectarian rigidity', although he does credit his theoretical outlook with being characterised by 'startling percipience', particularly in relation to his critique of social democracy and his original thinking regarding trade unionism.[15]

Evidently, De Leon made plenty of enemies. Those who have not detested him, however, have tended to worship him, often with an excess of idolatry which would not have embar-

5

rassed Stalin. For example, Henry Kuhn, National Secretary of the SLP from 1892 until 1906, outlived De Leon and contributed in 1919 to a pamphlet on De Leon's life; Kuhn's section was entitled 'Reminiscences of Daniel De Leon – Leader, Teacher, Pathfinder'. He asserts that:

> no sentient human being could have escaped being influenced by a personality such as De Leon's. His vast knowledge, made mobile and available by a virile mentality, the purity of his motives engendering a flawless devotion to the movement, his absolute fearlessness and steadfastness in the face of whatever might befall, never wavering, never faltering never perturbed . . . he was, indeed, a tower of strength. It was as though Providence had first shaped and then selected him as an instrument to hold aloft the banner of the Social Revolution at a time and during a period when, seemingly, no one else could have so held it.[16]

This, one should bear in mind, was supposed to be an account by a Marxist, who held that history is not made by 'Great Men' and not a chapter in *The Lives of the Saints*.

In 1923 Olive Johnson's article on De Leon in the *Modern Quarterly*, published in Baltimore, contained much that was of biographical and political interest, and also the suggestion that

> while the movement made De Leon, De Leon was also a powerful instrument in shaping the destiny of the American movement. Without his powerful mind and powerful influence the Socialist movement might, undoubtedly would, to a great extent . . . have run along the same channels as the general European Social Democracy, emasculated by reforms, compromise and log-rolling with capitalist parties.[17]

But the supreme admirer of De Leon – the man who saw it as his historic mission to elevate his dead leader into the gallery of Marxist deities – was Arnold Petersen, who was National Secretary of the SLP for fifty-five years from 1914 until 1969.

Amongst the vast number of pamphlets written by Petersen were *De Leon — The Uncompromising, Daniel De Leon — Orator, Daniel De Leon — Pioneer Socialist Editor, Daniel De Leon — Educator, Daniel De Leon — Internationalist, Daniel De Leon — Character Builder, Daniel De Leon — Disciplinarian* and many, many more. When one adds to these works of unrestrained praise those words of admiration for De Leon from characters ranging from Lenin, the Russian Bolshevik, to Bevan, the British Labour MP; from the anarchist, Guy Aldred, to Eugene Debs, the five-times socialist candidate for President — it becomes clear that we are looking at a complex historical figure.

So who was this Daniel De Leon, so reviled and respected with such intensity by so many people? He was born on 14 December 1852 on the Caribbean island of Curaçao, forty miles off the Venezuelan coast. The Dutch had first colonised the semi-arid island in 1634, and De Leon's father, Salomon, was a surgeon in the Dutch colonial army. The main economic value of Curaçao to the Netherlands was its participation in the slave trade. The abolition of slavery, by the Dutch King William III, in 1863, when De Leon was eleven, forced Curaçao into economic decline until the beginning of the twentieth century, when it became home for one of the world's largest oil refineries. The island has long-established Jewish, as well as Muslim, Protestant and Catholic communities, and De Leon was born into a family of Sephardic Jews. De Leon's reluctance to admit his Jewish origins was a response to widespread anti-Semitism from his opponents, including some who perpetrated the absurd allegation that his real name was Loeb, and that he and Henry Kuhn were owners of the Jewish banking company, Kuhn, Loeb and Company. Salomon De Leon, who was a prominent colonial government official as well as a diligent physician, died when Daniel was twelve, and was the first person to be buried in a new Jewish cemetery on

7

Curaçao. Daniel was looked after by his mother, Sarah, until 1866, when he was sent to Europe for the good of his health. De Leon could never tolerate a hot climate. On 15 April he sailed on a Norwegian ship from the Venezuelan port of Puerto Cabello and arrived in Hamburg on 22 May. At a Gymnasium in Hildesheim in the Hartz Mountains, he was given a broad education in the three-and-a-half-years before the Franco-Prussian War. In 1870 he moved to the prestigious University of Leyden in Holland, where there is evidence that he followed his father's footsteps in studying medicine. In 1872, at the age of twenty, De Leon returned to the USA, having become fluent in German, Spanish, Dutch, French, English, Greek and Latin – the latter being utilised well in later years in his frequent allusions to Roman history. It seems that he also acquired a reading knowledge of Italian, Portuguese and Modern Greek.

Back home, De Leon married Sarah Lobo, a Venezuelan. The couple had a conventional Jewish marriage. They moved into the Hispanic area of New York and, in 1883, had their first child, Salomon – generally known by his nickname of Solon. Their second son, Grover Cleveland, died before he was two years old. In 1886 De Leon's mother-in-law, who lived with the family, died; then on 29 April 1887 Sarah, his wife, died in pregnancy at the age of twenty-one – with her died two still-born twin sons. In five years since returning from Europe, Daniel De Leon had made a family and ended up with only one living son. He went to lodge with an Irish-woman, Mary Maguire, who looked after him and Solon.

As for employment, in 1874 De Leon was hired by Thomas B. Harrington's School in Wetchester County, where he taught Latin, Greek and Mathematics. In 1876 he went to study at Columbia University, obtaining his LLB two years later, as well as being awarded prizes for his essays on Constitutional

Law and International Law. In presenting these prizes Columbia's President Barnard made the prescient comment that 'Your successful labors afford ground for the just expectation that you may find your place among the distinguished publicists of the age and the country.'[18] In 1883 De Leon became a law lecturer at Columbia University. It has been alleged by De Leon's opponents that in the five years between 1878 and 1883 he worked in a private law practice.

In 1891, while on a socialist speaking tour, De Leon met his second wife, Bertha Canary. Before leaving on the tour, De Leon was advised by a friend to pay a visit to Independence, Kansas, where he believed some converts to the cause were waiting to be made. On his way back east from speaking in San Francisco, he arrived in Kansas and, finding that a meeting in Lawrence had been cancelled, he went to Independence, where he met the twenty-six-year-old Bertha, a schoolteacher who had fallen under the spell of Edward Bellamy's utopianism and formed a 'Christian Socialist Club'. On 23 April Bertha was delighted to meet De Leon, whose article on Marx in the pro-Bellamy journal she had read and admired. She wrote: 'We spent a pleasant hour and decided that the public meeting would have to be just the people I could get together in my home by personal invitation the coming Saturday evening. Twelve or fifteen people came and seemed very much interested, but no organization resulted.'[19] One year later the couple married in South Norwalk, Connecticut. They had five children, three girls and two boys. It was, by all accounts, a particularly happy marriage, with Bertha retaining her own views, despite the claims about her husband's intellectually dominating character.

So much for personal biography. How did De Leon, born into the colonial establishment in Curaçao, become De Leon the political revolutionary? According to Olive Johnson, who knew De Leon more intimately than most, he had been a social dissenter

9

even as a child. She tells the story of how, as a child on Curaçao, his family was informed that a slave had run away. 'What ingratitude', said an uncle. 'I sent that fellow some rum when he was ill' 'And I', said an Aunt, 'sent some extra food to his children only the other day.' 'But did anyone ever offer to give him his liberty?', a child's voice piped up., All eyes turned on that boy, and one of the party, looking at the boy's parents, said: 'I warn you, this boy will come to some bad end.'

The first clear political move by De Leon towards this 'bad end' came in the early 1870s, when he became an associate editor of a journal which advocated Cuban independence. It was not until 1886, when he was thirty-four years of age, that De Leon's radicalism impinged upon his daily life. From being a university law lecturer, concerned to achieve academic tenure, events pushed him into conflict with the status quo. In the spring of 1886 the horse-car workers in New York went on strike. So just were their grievances that even the city police refused to be used to break the strike. The city authorities sacked the recalcitrant police and hired some more workers in uniform with a brief to smash the strike by bringing the full strength of the law into force against the strikers. De Leon, the legal academic, read of the strike-breaking in his newspaper, but, according to Olive Johnson to whom he recounted the story, he did not bother about it with more than passing interest. Then the strikers won and organised a grand victory parade which passed Columbia College, which was located at that time on Madison Avenue, opposite St Patrick's Cathedral. Johnson describes what happened next:

> The street cars came in a row down the avenue. The workers had won. The group of professors hastened to the window and saw the parade go by. De Leon's colleagues expressed during this procession so much contempt and scorn and even threats against the workers that De Leon felt his blood boil.[20]

Aroused by the ignorant and embittered conservatism of his so-called intellectual colleagues, De Leon decided on which side he stood. More accurately, he decided on which side he did not stand: namely, on that of the capitalists and their academic hirelings. It was to take four more years of radical searching for answers before De Leon committed himself to the socialist cause. In those years his lecturing met with the response of the university authorities refusing to offer him tenure; by 1890 the message had been driven home and De Leon resigned his lectureship, never to return to university life. In later years De Leon was to reserve no fire in his attacks upon the role of universities – Columbia in particular. For example, when Professors Woodberry and MacDowell caused a scandal by resigning from Columbia University, De Leon wrote in the *Daily People* of 12 February 1904, that:

> As a factory is not run 'for the health' of its owners, as a newspaper is not operated 'for the fun' it affords its shareholders, neither is a privately owned 'institution of learning' conducted for 'patriotism'. Do not Professors Woodberry and MacDowell know that recently one of the Columbia University Professors – Munroe Smith – issued a circular call for money for the university addressed to millionaires, and there held language which amounts to this: "Share with us your wealth; it is a good investment; you need the blockheads whom we cultivate; if we do not addle the brains of these youths where would you be; shell out!"[21]

Between the dawning of De Leon's radicalised consciousness in 1886 and his emergence as a Marxian socialist in 1890, he fell under the sway of two powerful intellectual currents, both motivated by books which gave rise to popular American movements. The first was Henry George's *Progress and Poverty*, published in 1879. George's theory was compellingly simple: It was that society's most precious resource, land, is owned by landlords who parasitically expropriate rent from its users. As civilisation advances as a consequence of technical progress, poverty increases because the land becomes more valuable and the rents higher. To quote George:

> The reason why, in spite of the increase of productive power, wages constantly tend to a minimum which will give but a bare living, is that, with increase in productive power, rent tends to even greater increase, thus producing a constant tendency to the forcing down of wages.[22]

The solution would be a tax on rent. This would deny the benefits of increments in land values to the landlords and place such revenue in the public purse, thus alleviating poverty. This was the famous Henry George Single Tax Scheme. It appealed to small farmers in debt to big landlords, to some industrial capitalists who opposed their rivals whose capital was in land, to vast number of Irish immigrants whom historical experience had injected with a profound hatred for the evils of land-lordism, and to many urban workers, some hoping for a policy which would provide cheaper food. The scheme also appealed to some intellectuals, like De Leon, simply looking for a radical political alternative. Henry George's election campaign for the New York mayoralty in 1886 offered De Leon, the disillusioned academic, something for which to fight.

On 1 October De Leon addressed a pro-George rally. The New York *Tribune* reports him as speaking 'fluently', but with 'a strong French accent'. In fact, he spoke with a trace of a Spanish accent, including a slight lisp. Petersen described De Leon's oratory as 'a miracle of coherency, co-ordination and summation', but admitted that 'the tonal quality of his voice was neither rich nor sonorous. It could, and in fact did at times, become a falsetto . . .'.[23] Despite that, De Leon seems, from the outset, to have been a spellbinding orator. In his pro-George speech, De Leon showed his oratorical ability and growing class consciousness:

We have hitherto been ruled in this city by a small minority that have no interest whatever in our welfare. They are professional politicians whose headquarters are in the rum and grog shops, with points of vantage in the slums of our city, recruiting their strength from the criminal classes and in time swelling the ranks of those classes. These fellows do not care who is the nominee so long as he has money, and they await the result of all elections as the hungry wolves await carrion, for that is the time when their riotous carnival comes. It is not what brains or what common-sense or what capacity for government a man has, but what boo-dle he has.[24]

De Leon was not at this time a socialist, and when George rejected his socialist supporters in a bid to appear politically respectable, De Leon stuck with George. The latter was defeated by the Tammany Democratic candidate, Abram S. Hewitt, for whom George used to work as a speech-writer. Hewitt won 90,000 votes and George obtained 68,000, beating the Republican candidate, Theodore Roosevelt, who obtained 60,000 votes.

In 1888 Edward Bellamy published his technocratic utopia, *Looking Backward*, the story of a transformed, centralised and regimented USA in the year 2,000. By the end of 1889 it had sold 200,000 copies in the USA, making it the most popular utopian writing of modern times. Like George, Bellamy was no socialist. Indeed, the English Marxist, William Morris, was so appalled by Bellamy's vision, which he called a 'cockney par-adise', that he went away and wrote his own superb socialist utopian novel, *News From Nowhere* (1890). Bellamy's utopia arises not as a result of class struggle, but as a result of workers and capitalists alike seeing the sense of the new social arrangement.

Those who aimed to put Bellamy's scheme into action formed Nationalist clubs. By December 1889 there were 6,000 club members across the USA. De Leon became a Nationalist,

13

and it was this that brought him into contact with socialist ideas. The Nationalists of New York worked closely with the Socialistic Labor Party, the history of which is considered in the next chapter. Many Nationalist believed, like Bellamy, that 'all classes' could be won over to their movement. De Leon and the Left Bellamyites regarded Nationalism as being 'socialism by another name'. On 15 March 1890 De Leon wrote an article on Nationalism for the SLP's English-language newspaper, the *Workman's Advocate*. He described capitalist society as:

> a mob of warring individuals whose interests are hostile one to the other; while the establishment of the social system such as we are ripe for, and in which the land and the instruments of production should be held by the organised people and not by individuals for competitive strife, would transform us from mutual enemies into citizens; from a wild mob into a nation.

By the time of writing those words, De Leon had begun to read Marx under the guidance of the American-German Marxist, Hugo Vogt. In August 1889 he wrote an article for *The Nationalist* called 'The Voice of Madison', in which he showed some familiarity with Marx's law of value. It was only a matter of time before De Leon would formally become a socialist; on 25 September 1890 he joined the Socialistic Labor Party which he was to transform, dominate and remain in for the rest of his life.

2 The Socialist Labor Party

What was the Socialist Labor Party (SLP) which De Leon entered in 1890? It was the only socialist party in the USA, but where had it come from, and in what condition did De Leon find it?

Like the recipe for apple pie, Marxian socialist theory was imported to North America by European immigrants. Unlike apple pie, which has become a symbol of all that is American, socialist ideas were considered alien in a land which, despite being the home of primitive communist relations in centuries past, now came to be thought of as classless, free and without the need for obsolete European revolutionary doctrines. Undeterred, the European socialists advanced the case for world socialism. Two Marxists of German origin stand out as the principal carriers of European socialist ideas to the USA: Joseph Weydemeyer and Friedrich Albert Sorge.

Weydemeyer, a contemporary of Karl Marx, was urged by the latter to seek refuge in New York after the defeat of the 1848 revolution. He had previously worked with Marx in the Communist League and co-edited the *Neue Deutsche Zeitung*. He arrived in New York on 7 November 1851 and established the first-ever Marxist journal in the USA, *Die Revolution*. It ceased production after only two issues: New York German immigrants preferred to indulge in the romanticism of distant European nationalism than the scientific theorising of Marxism. Weydemeyer persisted. In 1852 he established the *Proletarier-*

bund, out of which came the American Workers' League, (AWL) the first Marxist organisation in the History of the USA. The inappropriately titled AWL – it was, in reality, a German Worker's League – adopted a declaration of principles calling for 'a firmly united and independent political party to assert and realise the rights of the workers. . . without respect to occupation, language, colour or sex'. The AWL collapsed in the mid-1850s, having failed to win to its ranks English-speaking – native, to use an inaccurate term – American workers.

Like Weydemeyer, Sorge was an exile from the defeated 1848 revolution in Germany. In fact, he did not want to face exile in the USA, first trying Switzerland, Belgium and England, and then boarding a boat for a new life in Australia – or so he thought, for the boat arrived in New York on 21 June 1852. Sorge was not a Marxist at this time and did not join the AWL, preferring to commit himself to preparations for a renewed 1848-style uprising and the discussion of Feuerbachian atheist humanism. It was after the Prussian defeat by Austria in the Six Weeks' War of 1866 that Sorge gave up waiting for this; he went over to Marxism and added his support to the recently formed International Working Men's Association (IWMA), the First International.

The First International created the first significant link between European and American socialists. It was essentially an international trade union solidarity movement, but socialists within it were intent upon internationalising the political struggle for socialism. In the USA William H. Sylvis formed the National Labor Union (NLU) in 1866, and as he became closer to socialist ideas he placed less emphasis on labour unions, regarding them as mere defensive bodies which make 'war upon the effects, leaving the cause undisturbed'. Sylvis concluded that 'the cause of all these evils is the 'WAGES SYSTEM',[1] i.e. the social system in which workers have to sell their mental and physical energies for a price in order to live. This coincided with Marx's view of the cause of the social evils, although Sylvis was not an orthodox Marxist. Sorge joined Local No. 5 of the NLU and, whilst unable to persuade the NLU to do so as a body, took Local No. 5 into the First International as Section One in the USA. By the early 1870's Marx's International had attracted a significant number of workers in the USA, including more than a few non-immigrant Americans. By 1872 twenty-two Sections of the International were able to assemble for a convention in New York.

Frustratingly, it was the recruitment into the First International of 'genuine' Americans that led to a split in the American organisation. This was almost entirely caused by a crankish crowd in Sections Nine and Twelve, dominated by the self-consciously demagogic Stephen Pearl Andrews and the eccentric sisters, Clafflin and Woodhull. Samuel Gompers, President of the AFL, who was never a Marxist of any description, looked upon these 'faddists, reformers and sensation-loving spirits' of Sections Nine and Twelve as a detestable aberration: 'Those pseudo-communists played with the labor movement', he rightly observed.[2] This was not the last time that the American socialist movement would be blighted by the theoretically superficial and politically utopian schemes of reformers whose numbers expanded the movement but at an unacceptable price. By the 1870s the International was being torn apart in Europe by the conflict between Marxists and followers of Bakunin; the General Council was moved to New York, with Sorge as General Secretary, but it was a dying movement and on 15 July 1876 Sorge and his comrades in Section One signed the death certificate.

The International had put socialism on the American political agenda, albeit somewhere near the bottom. On Independence Day, 1874, the Social Democratic Working Men's Party of

North America was formed. On 19 July 1876 several prominent American socialists convened in Philadelphia to form a united, independent socialist party. Out of the Philadelphia Conference came the Working Men's Party of the United States, with a membership of 2,500. At the party's second Convention in Newark, New Jersey, in December 1877, the name was changed to the Socialistic Labor Party – an adaptation of the Germanic *Sozialistische Arbeiter Partei* (the name was later changed to the more Americanised Socialist Labor Party). By the end of the decade the SLP had 10,000 members in one hundred Sections in twenty-five states. It had twenty-four party newspapers, eight of which were in English. The growth of the party was stimulted by two waves of European immigrants: German socialists fleeing from Bismarck's 1878 Anti-Socialist Laws; and, to a far lesser extent, refugees from the defeated Paris Commune of 1871.

The pre-1890, pre-De Leon SLP was anything but a party of clear-cut Marxian principles. In some states its members allied themselves with greenback currency reformers. In 1886 the SLP joined the United Labor Party in Henry George's mayoralty campaign. For their efforts, George disowned the socialists in 1887: he went on to political defeat and obscurity; some SLPers went on to oppose pragmatic alliances. But most did not, as is evident from a resolution carried at the Sixth National Convention of the SLP held in Buffalo, New York in 1887, which recommended to members that 'wherever one or more labor parties are in the field, to support the party which is the most progressive; that is, the platform and principles of which comes nearest to ours, and at least recognises the conflict between capital and labour. . .'. At the same time, some SLPers were adherents of the German, Ferdinand Lasalle, who preached the futility of all trade union action because wages are fixed by iron laws of capitalist value which cannot be amended by struggle. Others still contended that the SLP should work only within the labour unions, electoral activity being a waste of time. In 1889 an internal battle was raging over control of the administration of this confused little party and, after a National Convention was held in Chicago, the headquarters were moved from Manhattan to Brooklyn, and a new National Secretary was appointed, Benjamin J. Gretsch. It was into such political disarray that Daniel De Leon entered enthusiastically in September 1890.

De Leon's enthusiasm was twofold. First, he had at last discovered the socialist alternative and advanced beyond his 1886 position of merely hating society as it was. Secondly, De Leon had plans to modernise the SLP, to make it organisationally firm and politically clear. Specifically, De Leon sought to Americanise the Marxian socialist message, to strengthen its propaganda tactics, and to introduce discipline into the SLP's organisation and thinking. It is important to comprehend why these objectives meant so much to De Leon, and how far he accomplished them.

The first problem to confront De Leon in the SLP was that it was a European-dominated party in a non-European society. It was a party of aliens and it alienated American workers. When De Leon joined the SLP two members of its National Executive Committee (NEC) could speak English. They were Gretsch, a Russian student of law; and Henry Kuhn, who was to succeed him as De Leon's chosen National Secretary. Kuhn was a member of the Bookbinders' Union and an SLPer since the mid-1880s. De Leon was welcomed by this largely immigrant, artisan body, who were impressed by the fact that a learned professor had decided to join their ranks. Despite his Caribbean origin and slightly foreign accent, De Leon was seen as a real American, who used English better than most Americans and had a feel for American political life. Part of this 'feel' was a recognition that Marxian socialism would never receive a fair hearing from American workers as long as it seemed like a European doctrine. In 1887 this had been comprehended by Friedrich Engels, who wrote that the SLP had an important role to play, but 'in order to do so they will have to doff every remnant of their foreign garb. They will have to become out and out American'.[3] De Leon saw this American-isation of the movement as a fundamental necessity. It involved the need for more SLP propaganda material in English, but primarily it required socialists to work within the labour unions, where the workers were clearly combining, and push socialism as a native creed.

Unlike Marx, who was typical of most European thinkers in regarding the American political tradition and economic condition as infertile soil for imminent socialist growth, De Leon thought that both of these factors made the socialist task easier in the USA. He saw the democratic ideology which underlay American capitalism as a genuinely radical tradition of which socialist ideas were a logical culmination. Naive as it might seem, and perhaps explicable by De Leon's years as a scholar of the Constitution, he had genuine respect for the principles of the Revolutionary Fathers. He suggested that 'if Franklin lived today and the revolutionary fathers, they would realise that what they imagined would be the means of freedom had become the means of oppression'.[4] Indeed, it is the socialist, according to De Leon, who is the real patriot: 'Socialism is that idea that alone can raise patriotism to its completest development.'[5] As we shall see, De Leon was no gullible social democrat, believing in the neutrality of the state or the possibility of democratic rhetoric reflecting anything more than an ideological front for minority class rule under capitalism, but neither did he underestimate the American democratic aspiration. Those, like Algie Simons, who dismissed such aspiration as a mere sham, were regarded by De Leon as 'dry-as-dust dogmatists, whose Socialism goes by rote'.[6] Again, De Leon favoured socialists using what he called 'civilised methods' of winning the battle for socialism. Immigrant notions of insurrectionism, which may have had their place in European struggles against recalcitrant feudal forces, had no place in the American context.

De Leon did not share Marx's pessimism about the economic conditions making it unlikely for a socialist movement to grow in the USA. In short, Marx's view was that the Western frontier existed as a means of escape from regimented life as urban, industrial proletarians and gave American workers a sense of individualism and the potential to opt out of the class struggle. Although only a temporary historical phenomenon, this would impede the spread of socialist ideas. for De Leon, the USA was the place where the world socialist revolution would most likely start. He first stated this in 1894 and persisted in the belief with certainty: 'The fact is that the storm center will be here and not in Europe, and that America will lead, not follow. . . .'.[7] In the USA capitalism was developing fast and naked in its ugliness. Unlike in Europe, where the socialist struggle was side-tracked into conflicts against feudal forces, the battle in the USA would be a straight one between unadulterated capitalism and socialism: 'Economic and political development have gone on in a way that clears the field in America as it clears it in no other country under the sun.'[8]

In order to take advantage of the American situation, De Leon needed to free the SLP's propaganda from domination by those whom Engels had derided as German *Knoten*, i.e. narrow-minded philistines. In Engels's view, the exile of these German socialists by Bismarck's Anti-Socialist Laws was 'a misfortune not for Germany, but for America'.[9] When De Leon joined the SLP, it was not only lacking political clarity regarding its own aims but also absent was any strategy for action. The mainly

German membership had '[shrunk] – into social clubs – singing and drinking and card-playing societies, with an occasional outing when a member dies, and periodical celebrations in which thrilling speeches were delivered by themselves to themselves'.[10]

De Leon's main propaganda objective was to integrate socialism and trade unionism. (This is considered in the next chapter.) In addition, he set himself three other tasks. The first was to provide the SLP with a powerful English-language newspaper. When he joined in 1890, the party had two newspapers: *Der Sozialist*, which was in German and was edited by the experienced Marxian theorist, Hugo Vogt; and the *Workman's Advocate*, which was a four-page English broadsheet. In order to finance a larger, more widely circulated socialist newspaper in English, De Leon persuaded the SLP to organise a massive fund-raising picnic in 1890. In April 1891 the *People* was launched. It was edited by Lucien Sanial, a French ex-naval officer who had come to the USA after being active in the French socialist movement. De Leon was appointed as Sanial's assistant editor, the latter being twenty years older and more experienced. When Sanial's eyesight failed, De Leon became editor, in 1891. He retained the editorship for twenty-three years, working for all of that time without any paid journalistic staff, but relying at all times on volunteer writers to fill the space.

How did De Leon see the function of a socialist newspaper? He summed it up as follows:

A daily Socialist paper in the English language. . . must start with the knowledge that, in point of what is called news, it cannot think of competing with the capitalist contemporaries. . . An English Socialist daily may not trim its sails to attract 'new readers'; in that field it is *hors de combat* from the start; it must furnish a specialized kind of news that the capitalist press either does not care for, or does not want – legitimate, labor and social news; it must thus create a field from which capitalist competition is, *ipso facto*, excluded. With such a news policy, supplemented by a news policy that illustrates Socialist principles by the light of the events of the day, and watching its opportunity to enlarge, a daily social-ist paper must begin with modest aspirations. It must realise that ninety-nine out of every hundred of its readers will stick to the Egyptian fleshpots of the capitalist 'news' papers. It must aim at getting these readers to acquire a taste for its own bill of fare, without expecting them to drop their own favorite capitalist news menu, at least not immediately. It must thus slowly build up its own audience, upon its own ground. It must, in short, follow the tactics, not of attempting to dispute their field with the capitalist 'news' contemporaries, but, first, of seeking to share their read-ers; and then, as an ultimate aim, to strip them of their proletari-an dupe-audience, together with those in sympathy with these. Even such a course will encounter serious financial obstacles. But these obstacles it is possible to overcome.[11]

Without doubt, the *People* did avoid the trap of compromise for the sake of increasing readership. It did endure financially without advertising, although SLP records show that this was frequently at the cost of De Leon, as editor, being unpaid. The paper never reached mass circulation, with the difficulties imposed by the vastness of the USA and the paper's lack of access to the major newspaper distribution companies. According to the audits available, the *People*'s peak circulation was 13,500, in 1900. On 1 July of that year, the SLP resolved to turn it into a daily newspaper, a move which Henry Kuhn opposed at the time, and which seems almost certainly to have been a project too great for the small party (of about 1,500 at that time) to have loaded upon themselves. De Leon undertook the task with energetic enthusiasm, writing a staggering num-ber of over three-and-a-half thousand articles and editorials during his editorship. Kuhn believed that the establishment of the *Daily People* was the cause of the SLP losing members, who, 'unable to stand the strain drop away, thereby intensifying the burden carried by those who refuse to quit'.[12] None the less, the *People*, as a party-owned newspaper, with a party-appointed and accountable editor, proved a significant propaganda gain for the SLP.

De Leon was much aided in his plans for the SLP's written propaganda by the party's ownership of the New York Labor News Company (NYLN), established in 1887 as the first socialist publishing house in the USA. (Although Charles H. Kerr Co. was founded a year earlier, it did not begin to concentrate on socialist publications until 1900.) The possession of a printing press enabled the SLP to respond quickly to developments requiring socialist comment, and to do so without the constraints imposed by commercial printing. Furthermore, the NYLN could retain plates of printed matter, allowing the SLP to reprint successful pamphlets many times. The press was also used to produce the party's several foreign-language newspapers.

English translations of Marx's major writings were made available for the first time in the USA through the NYLN. De Leon himself translated Marx's *Eighteenth Brumaire of Louis Napoleon* and the *Critique of the Gotha Programme*, which he considered to be a work of fundamental strategic insight. The NYLN published Engels's *Socialism: From Utopia to Science*, translated by De Leon and with an introduction by Sanial. Also to be found in a list of recommended NYLN books from 1903 are translations by De Leon of Karl Kautsky's *The Working Class, The Capitalist Class, The Class Struggle* and *The Socialist Republic*; Sanial's *Socialist Almanac* as well as books by him on taxation and trusts; Belfort Bax's *Short History of the Paris Commune*; James Connolly's *Erin's Hope*; William Scholl McClure's lecture on *Socialism*; and speeches by De Leon. One of De Leon's most interesting translations from German

Marxism was of August Bebel's *Woman Under Socialism*, the contents of which were to feature later in the dispute with Connolly.

De Leon did not confine his translation work to political ideas. Like Morris in England, he saw no incompatibility between an enthusiasm for the literary arts and political education. He translated Ferdinand Lassalle's little-known play, *Franz von Sickingen*, and from French he translated, and the NYLN published, the epic series of novels by Eugene Sue called *The Mysteries of the People*, or *History of a Proletarian Family Across the Ages*. In his preface to *The Gold Sickle*, the first of the nineteen novels, De Leon describes *The Mysteries* as

> a series of stories, supposedly written from age to age, sometimes at shorter, other times at longer intervals, by the descendants of the ancestral type of the oppressed, narrating their special experience and handling the supplemented chronicle known to their successors from generation to generation.. . The series, accordingly, though a work presented in the garb of 'fiction', is the best universal history extant: Better than any work, avowedly on history, it graphically traces the special features of class-rule as they succeeded one another from epoch to epoch.[13]

De Leon believed that 'the usurping class in the English-speaking world' had 'succeeded in keeping this brilliant torch that Eugene Sue lighted, from casting its rays across the path of the English-speaking world'.[14] Whatever else De Leon can be credited with achieving, or charged with destroying, there can be no denying his success in pioneering in the USA the dissemination of Marxist and radical literature in English, ranging from the *People* to pamphlets to novels.

De Leon's second propaganda objective was to take the SLP beyond the immigrant margins of New York and transform it into a national party. In 1891 he was sent on a speaking tour which extended as far west as the Pacific coast. In an age in which television or radio did not exist, the force of the orator, on the public platform, at the street meeting or in open debate was the most powerful means of communicating ideas. De Leon's oratory was magnificent. The stenographic records of his most important speeches (most of De Leon's principal works are, in fact, transcripts of speeches) demonstrate the immense logical force and the eloquence he commanded. Lacking the emotive power of Debs or the romantic charisma of 'Big' Bill Haywood, and perhaps slightly impeded by his Spanish accent, De Leon's main rhetorical weapon seems to have been the authority of being learned. He was a man who inspired fear in opponents and reverence from friends. Perhaps this apparently 'natural' authority came from his early conditioning into a life of privilege; perhaps from a professorial confidence which disarmed those who had never encountered the arrogance of the university style; but also, it most certainly emanated from the evident intellectual clarity which characterised the De Leon speaking and writing style. According to Arnold Petersen:

> He would lay down his major premise, and then support it with a battery of facts, and a logic so all-compelling that one had the extraordinary sensation of having had one's previous views and conceptions completely clarified and confirmed, though in all probability what had really happened was that De Leon, with that mastery of simple and direct statement and overwhelming logic that was his, had succeeded in planting one or more new ideas in the minds of his listeners.[15]

De Leon' 1891 speaking tour transformed the SLP from a New York-based immigrant club of approximately 1,500 members into a national organisation with one hundred Sections and Locals.

It was this work of making socialists which laid the groundwork for De Leon's third objective for the SLP: electoral activity. He rejected those SLP members who saw the party as

26

a vehicle for abstract propagandism, an institute for the study of political theory. As we shall see, De Leon was no electoral fetishist, but he did see the importance of political activity in the contest for state power as being essential to demonstrating the credibility of the SLP as a party. After his 1891 national tour, De Leon ran as SLP candidate for governor of New York. He won 13,000 votes. A year earlier the SLP candidate for mayor of New York, August Delabar, polled 5,000 votes. Compared to the votes polled by the capitalist candidates, these were negligible but they were the first-ever socialist votes cast in the USA, and the fact that there were thousands of them gave cause for enthusiastic optimism.

In 1892 the SLP felt confident enough to nominate a presidential ticket, which appeared on the ballot in the states of New York, New Jersey, Pennsylvania, Connecticut and Massachusetts. Simon Wing ran for President, with Charles H. Matchett as Vice-President. They received 21,173 votes. In 1896 the SLP' national votes increased to 36,367, and in 1898 reached a peak of 82,204. From then it declined to 33,382 in 1900, 33,510 in 1904, 14,029 in 1908 and 29,213 in 1912, the year that Debs won a staggering 897,011 votes on the basis of an undisguisedly militant manifesto. In 1892 the SLP's 21,000 plus votes looked like the beginning of the growth of American workers' political consciousness. Frank Katz, an SLPer and activist in the Cigar Makers' Union, recalled that after the 1892 campaign, the *'People* gained in circulation and prestige, and began to reach and be appreciated by workingmen even in other English-speaking countries.The virile, clearcut, logical and inimitable style of its editor differed as much from previous writings in Socialist papers . . . as a piano differs from the tom-tom of the savage.' Indeed, 'Sections began to sprout up everywhere, and Daniel De Leon was hailed as the man to raise high the banner of Socialism in America.'[16] So, within two years in the SLP De Leon had succeeded in establishing himself as editor of a weekly newspaper in English, spreading the geographical range of the SLP, and making an electoral impact with revolutionary socialist politics. In short, he had transformed the propaganda work of the SLP.

Having Americanised and strengthened the propagandist impact of the party, De Leon had one other, objective to which he attached the greatest importance. The SLP had to be turned into a party of cast-iron revolutionary principles, in which members would adhere to a code of socialist conduct based upon a recognition of the imperative need for organisational unity.

For De Leon, the socialist organisation could not be a 'broad church'. His first decade of activity in the SLP convinced him that "Broadness" had been a bane. . . no party can expect to accomplish anything that turns itself into an ash-barrel for the refuse of all others.'[17] In the 1890s the Populists courted SLP alliance, particularly in the west, but De Leon regarded growth in numbers at the expense of principles as a dangerous and unacceptable course. Even within the SLP, those opponents of Marxian theoretical orthodoxy and organisational uniformity were treated as suspect by De Leon and the majority who adhered to his position. As one SLP member wrote to De Leon, 'In order for the SLP to do good work I believe it is absolutely necessary to keep it *pure.*' Daniel De Lury wrote to De Leon on 23 February 1897, expressing his view that 'at this time we need an "intolerant", "tyrannical" paper to keep the movement in line.'[18] De Leon contended that the co-operative nature of the socialist movement necessitates collective unity. In 'Reform or Revolution', which is the text of De Leon's speech to the socialists of Boston, given in 1896, advising them to adopt the SLP-style principles of the New York socialists, he outlined his reasoning thus:

The Socialist. . . sees that the lone fiddler in his room needs no director; he can rap himself to order, with his fiddle to his shoulder, and start his dancing tune and stop whenever he likes. But as soon as you have an orchestra, you must also have an orchestra director – a central directing authority. If you don't you may have a Salvation army powwow, you may have a Louisiana Negro breakdown; you may have an orthodox Jewish synagogue, where every man sings in whatever key he likes, but you won't have harmony – impossible. It needs this central directing authority of the orchestra master to rap all the players to order at a given moment. . . The orchestra director is not an oppressor, nor is his baton an insignia of tyranny; he is not there to bully anybody; he is as necessary or important as any or all the members of the orchestra.[19]

This raises the question of who or what the 'central directing authority' is to be. If it is to be a leadership concentrated in a person – namely, De Leon – then the common allegations by the SLP's opponents of De Leon's 'bossism' would be valid. But De Leon did not see himself as a director, above or apart from the SLP. Neither did the SLP members who, according to Joao Claudino, objected to 'the impression that Daniel De Leon is the whole Socialist Labour Party – that the rank and file are nothing but a set of idiots or crazy fanatics. . .'. He pointed out that 'Mr De Leon is a member of the SLP who enjoys no more privileges than the rest of the class conscious membership.'[20] To the extent that De Leon was looked up to by other socialists this was a consequence of his exceptional abilities rather than any tyrannical ambitions. For De Leon, the authority to which all members must conform was the principled unity of the organisation.

In 'Reform or Revolution', De Leon stated five obligations which all socialists must accept. First, s/he is required to 'work in organisation with all that that implies.' There can be no freelance revolutionaries, operating independently of the

party. De Leon attacks 'the reformer' who 'spurns organisation; his symbol is "Five Sore Fingers on a Hand" – far apart
from one another'. Socialists recognise that only in unity is
there strength. Secondly, socialists know 'full well that man is
not superior to principle, that principle is superior to man' and
that 'organization must be the incarnation of principle'.
Thirdly, 'you will ever see the revolutionist submit to the will
of the majority. . . you will never find the revolutionist
putting himself above the organization'. From this follows a
fourth revolutionary characteristic, which is that s/he is prepared to couple 'individual freedom' with 'collective freedom',
the latter involving democratic adherence to 'a central directing authority'. The unity of the political whole would have to
be at the cost of the autonomy of its parts. Fifthly, the revolutionist exhibits 'consistency' and 'is truthful'.[21]

How far did De Leon live up to these standards? He was
certainly an organisation man: he joined the SLP in 1890 and
remained in it, without any lapse of activity or apparent
thought of resignation, until he died. He did not try to elevate
himself above the principles which he espoused, or use the
principles in any opportunist way. De Leon did submit to the
majority will. Despite the allegations of personal tyranny or
'bossism', the record demonstrates that De Leon enjoyed no
power within the SLP to which he was not elected, and made
no decisions alone but as a result of winning majority support.
This does not, in itself, dispose of all charges regarding his
authoritarianism.De Leon was a person who placed a possibly
unhealthy emphasis on the significance of his own judgements,
and he did entertain excessive suspicions, sometimes bordering
on the paranoid, about plots to divert the SLP from his leadership. In turn, these characteristics were partly justified. De
Leon's supreme confidence in himself may not have been arrogance but a realistic assessment that he was a clearer thinker

and better organiser than anyone else in the SLP. The suspicious mentality may have resulted partly from the hypersensitivity of a leader who did not like people who answered back, but the much greater evidence is that it resulted from the genuine strain of trying to keep a party of principles intact in the face of repeated plots to undermine its revolutionary nature. In short, the question of De Leon's 'bossism' is more complicated than is allowed for by the glib charges which have often been repeated by historians. Whatever the case, De Leon was not an anti-democrat. He did accept centralised authority in the SLP; for example, as editor of the *People* he was controlled by, and accountable to, the National Executive Committee (NEC). In 1904 there was an SLP ballot on whether to retain him as editor, which he won by 824 to four votes. On the fifth standard outlined in 'Reform or Revolution', De Leon's reputation is less certain. Was he consistent in his ideas? He certainly remained a Marxist, but his ideas did change, sometimes quite sharply. For example, as will be shown in the next chapter, his position on trade unionism zig-zagged considerably. Was De Leon truthful? Connolly was to claim that De Leon conducted his polemic against him dishonestly, and others were to suggest that, in support of his position on trade unions, he made dishonest use of a quotation from Marx which was of dubious origin. In general, it can be stated that De Leon checked his facts meticulously, always stating his case against capitalism with impeccable honesty.

De Leon imposed these standards of revolutionary conduct upon the SLP. Membership of the party was not automatic, but depended on a requirement for applicants to demonstrate their acceptance of SLP principles. The price paid for this was a smaller party than De Leon's rejected 'ash-barrel for the refuse of all others' would have been. That this was a human price, paid for in frustration and occasional despondency, can be seen from the letter sent by T. J. Dean, the Washington State Organiser, to Henry Kuhn, the National Secretary, on 18 January 1897:

> I was certain I had a doz[en] men who were in earnest and would go into the movement . . . they were all ready to sign when the pledge to sever connection with other political parties met their eyes and the result was they were not ready to sign. In other words they were not yet sufficiently socialistic to be socialists. Understand me – I had an expression from each of them that they were opposed to wage slavery . . . and [that] the only way to eradicate it was through the co-operative ownership of the means of production, distribution and exchange. All had agreed that it must be an international movement and all seemed to have a class consciousness.
>
> Well when all but 4 or 3 of them refused to sign I felt like sobing [*sic*]. That men can come so close and yet be so far from triumph is hard to bear.

Such men would not have been refused membership of the British ILP in 1897 for refusing to break their links with other parties. Was this dogmatic sectarianism, for which De Leon can be attacked? Or rather, was the SLP insisting on basic principles of socialist conduct, without which a movement for socialism becomes one in name only? Upon the answer to these questions depends the assessment of De Leon's role in moulding the first Marxist party in the USA.

3 Trade unionism and the abolition of the wages system

One passage by Marx provided the basis for De Leon's thinking about the uses and limitations of trade unionism:

> quite apart from the general servitude involved in the wages system, the working class ought not to exaggerate to themselves the ultimate working of these everyday struggles. They ought not to forget that they are fighting with effects, but not with the causes of those effects; that they are retarding the downward movement, but not changing its direction; that they are applying palliatives, not curing the malady. They ought, therefore, not to be exclusively absorbed in these unavoidable guerrilla fights incessantly springing up from the never-ceasing encroachments of capital or changes of the market. They ought to understand that, with all the miseries it imposes upon them, the present system simultaneously engenders the material conditions and the social forms necessary for an economic reconstruction of society. Instead of the conservative motto, 'A fair day's wages for a fair day's work!' they should inscribe on their banner the revolutionary watchword, 'Abolition of the wages system!'[1]

This did not constitute a proposal for workers to abandon the trade-union struggle, but it did urge workers to see the limited value of such partial, defensive activity. This was De Leon's view. He recognised the inevitability of strikes under capitalism. Indeed, he was encouraged by them, for 'The slave . . . who will not rise against his master . . . is hopeless. But the slave who. . . persists, despite failures and poverty, in rebelling, there is always hope for.'[2] De Leon's fear was that this hope, arising out of the exciting spontaneity of struggle, would be seen by workers as a sufficient means of guaranteeing their security. Like Marx, De Leon saw such efforts to obtain economic fairness under the profit system as an ever-repeating process based on a fundamentally conservative assumption that capitalism can deliver genuine justice.

In order to summarise fully De Leon's early attitude towards trade unionism, it will be useful to look closely at a speech which he gave to the striking textile workers of New Bedford, Massachusetts in 1898. He was invited to address them as the leading figure in the only socialist party in the USA, the SLP. His speech published and republished many times since under the title 'What Means This Strike?' captures De Leon's masterful ability to simplify socialism in compelling terms. It was arguably his finest achievement as a propagandist.

De Leon began by mocking the custom which prevailed then, as now, when major strikes are taking place, for 'stars' in the labor movement' to be invited to 'entertain the strikers . . . with rosy promises and prophesies, funny anecdotes, bombastic recitations in prose and poetry. . .'. These leaders come to boost the workers' spirits, 'much in the style that some generals do, who, by means of bad whiskey, seek to keep up the courage of the soldiers whom they are otherwise unable to beguile'.[3] So, was De Leon opposed to attempts to raise morale during strikes? He was not, but he was opposed to building false hopes and exaggerating the effectiveness of defensive trade union action. De Leon told the strikers that he had not come to patronise them with rhetoric but in order to show why strikes occur and how real victory could be achieved.

De Leon started his explanation by addressing the fallacy that the capitalists, by paying wages, support the workers. In simple stages, De Leon demonstrated that the reverse is true:

the workers produce all of the wealth, but receive only a fraction of it back as wages: 'the profits that the capitalist pockets represent wealth that the wage workers produced and that the capitalist . . . steals from them'.[4] He compared the accumulation of profits by the capitalists to the biblical story about manna being sent from Heaven to feed the Jews when they were in the wilderness. The capitalist can lie flat on his back all day and night and, like manna from Heaven, his dividends come to him because 'profits are the present and running stealings perpetrated by the capitalist upon the workingman" and 'capital is the accumulated past stealings of the capitalist'.[5]

Having shown that it is the workers, by taking wages and giving profits, who support the capitalists, and not the other way round, De Leon proceeded to explain the inevitable antagonism of interests – or class struggle – which necessarily ensues:

> A thing cannot be divided into two shares so as to increase the share of each. If the workingman produces, say, $4 worth of wealth a day, and the capitalist keeps 2, there are only 2 left for the workingman; if the capitalist keeps 3 there is only 1 left for the workingman. . . Inversely, if the workingman pushes up his share from $1/2$ to 1, there are only 3 left to the capitalist . . . if the workingman push [*sic*] still onward and keep 3, the capitalist will have to put up with 1 – and if the workingman makes up his mind to enjoy all that he produces, and keep all 4, THE CAPITALIST WILL HAVE TO GO TO WORK.[6]

So, unless the workers are to be robbed on precisely the capitalist's terms, and until they are to demand the full fruits of their labour, a hostile struggle is unavoidable: 'No glib-tongued politician can vault over it, no capitalist professor or official statistician can argue it away; no capitalist parson can veil it; no labor faker can straddle it; no "reform" architect can bridge it over.'[7]

35

The last part of 'What Means This Strike?' is devoted to the question of how to 'organize so as not to fight the same old hopeless battles'.[8] De Leon outlines three basic principles; after 1904 these would be elaborated upon when he devised his later position, socialist Industrial Unionism (which is considered in Chapter 5), but in the 1890s he confined himself to simpler conclusions. First, the organised workers must realise that they will never be safe until capitalism, with its private ownership of the productive machinery, has been overthrown and a system of collective ownership established. This is not to suggest that improvements should not be struggled for under capitalism, but that this struggle should not be undertaken with any illusion that it will leave the workers secure. Secondly, labour organisations must accept that politics is a matter for collective concern, just as wages are. For De Leon, politics is not a matter to be left to the conscience of each worker, in the way that religious belief is. The economic struggle and the political struggle are inseparable. 'For the same reason that the organization of labor . . . execrates the scab in the shop, it must execrate the scab at the hustings.'[9] Thirdly, the labour organisation not only rejects capitalist politicians, but rejects all politicians and instead votes for principles. The only 'platform and program' worthy of principled support, asserts De Leon, is 'THE ABOLITION OF THE WAGES SYSTEM OF SLAVERY'.[10]

De Leon was not advocating new ideas. His principal concern was to apply the orthodox position of Marx to the industrial conditions of his own time, and to simplify its reasoning and conclusions. In this sense, De Leon was not amongst the original theoreticians of socialism, but more in the category of Robert Tressell or William Morris, whose talent lay in popularising what might otherwise have remained dusty, scholarly formulas. The idea of abolishing wage labour was neither new nor idealistically frightening to many American workers in the

1890s. We have already observed that in 1869, Sylvis's view of American society in the 'gilded age' was that 'The cause of all these evils is the WAGES SYSTEM.' Indeed, from the massively popular impact of Bellamy's vision of a society without wages, to the rugged individualism of the frontier mentality which would never be degraded into the slave bondage of wage labour so long as an independent living could be made, there was something central to the American people's view of their own liberty and dignity which abhorred wage labour. In 1893 the English socialists issued the *Manifesto of English Socialists*, which called for the abolition of wage labour, but this was never to have such an impact in a concentratedly urbanised society, where the wealth producers had been conditioned by generations of feudal and semi-feudal rulers to know their place. In the USA of the 1890s industrial capitalism was a much mistrusted animal.

It is necessary to put to rest one long-standing myth about De Leon's theory of wages. It has been asserted that he accepted the Lassallean 'iron law of wages'. Lassalle argued that 'the average wage always remains reduced to the necessary subsistence which is required by the people according to its habits, for the maintenance of existence and reproduction'.[11] In short, the value of labour power is fixed and cannot be altered by struggle. The same view was put by 'Citizen Weston', a member of the First International, and the so-called 'iron law' was refuted by Marx in 1865 in his *Value, Price and Profit*. Lassalle's theory, which involved the dismissal of all trade union struggle as being futile, did make an impression on the socialists of the USA. Indeed, when De Leon joined the SLP, amongst all of the many areas of confusion about its position, there was a raging conflict between the Marxists like Hugo Vogt, who saw the need for trade unions as defensive bodies, and a Lassallean wing which did not. The myth that De Leon was a Lassallean seems to have arisen in Leninist circles. In his book, *Marx and America*, the American Communist Party (CPUSA) leader, Earl Browder, refers to 'the insistence of early American socialists upon a dogmatic subsistence-wage theory (or even upon the "iron law" in the case of De Leon and the Lassalleans)'.[12] Another CPUSA member, Carl Reeve, claims that De Leon 'preached that under capitalism, struggles for wage increases, strikes, actions for shorter hours and of the economic demands... were worse than useless, since, in any case, workers receive for their labor no more than that which was needed for existence and reproduction'.[13] Recently, one Leninist sect in the USA has pronounced that 'the impact of De Leon's teachings – because of his misunderstanding of the factors determining the value of labor power (i.e. his "iron law of wages") – was to keep revolutionaries out of the class struggle and preach to the working class the *renunciation* of its struggle against its mortal enemy, capital',[14] In fact, De Leon did not adhere to the iron law of wages; he vigorously opposed it and exposed the errors of Lassalle. Three pieces of evidence demonstrate this fact. The first is that it was De Leon himself who translated into English for the first time Marx's *Value, Price and Profit* – the classical statement in refutation of the iron law. It would be rather odd for a propagandist to translate, publish and distribute a work written to show the falsity of his own thinking. Secondly, as we shall see, De Leon was an active trade unionist from 1890 until his death. Why would a Lassallean, committed to a belief in the inefficacy of strikes, spend as much time as De Leon did advocating millitant trade unionism? Thirdly, and most convincingly, it is clear that De Leon rejected the iron law of wages because he said so quite explicitly. For example, in reply to a Lassallean correspondent in the *Weekly People* on 20 February 1909, De Leon states that 'the Socialist movement has long ago discarded his [i.e. Lassalle's] "Iron Lawe of Wages" as untenable' and that the theory had been thrown 'on the rubbish heap of exploded notions'. Again, in the *Daily People* of 18 February 1910, in one of his many attacks upon Thomas E. Watson, the Southern Populist leader, he points out that Watson is wrong in stating that Marx ever adhered to the iron law of wages, or that the term has an application to Marxian economic theory. He goes on:

> the 'iron law of wages' is known in economics mainly through Lassalle. . . According to his theory, seeing that supply and demand regulate prices, workingmen, being many, wages would go down; the privations that lower wages would bring about, would also bring about a decrease of proletarians; the decreased supply of workers would then bring wages up; the prosperity of higher wages would then result in an increase of proletarians; the increased supply would thereupon bring wages down again, back to where they were – and so on, in an endless, vicious and unbreakable circle. This Lassalle called the 'iron law of wages'. It is partly made up of Malthusianism. It is untrue. It is rejected by Socialists. No Socialist talks of the 'iron law of wages'.

Given that De Leon did recognise the power of trade union struggle as a means of improving wages and conditions, it is no surprise that, despite the limitations of trade unionism, he supported such action. There was another reason why De Leon wanted socialists to be working in the labour unions. The unions were where organised workers could be found. Their membership was rising: the American Federation of Labor (AFL) had 130,000 members when it was formed in 1886. By 1897 it had 440,000 members, and 1,598,000 by 1905. This union membership was concentrated rather than being scattered nationally: in 1890 half of the urban population of the USA lived in the five states of New York, Pennsylvania, Massachusetts, Illinois and Ohio. Once inside the unions, working alongside other workers, socialists could push forward the socialist case for abolishing the wages system. Indeed, De Leon attached great importance not only to making socialist ideas known within the labour unions, but also to winning socialist control of the trade union movement. With this in view, the SLP embarked in 1890 on a campaign of 'boring from within'.

There were two major union bodies in the USA to be infiltrated: one, the Knights of Labor (K of L), was militant and declining; the other, the AFL, was conservative and expanding. The SLP entered both, with De Leon concentrating on the K of L.

The AFL was a body of craft unions, more interested in defending skilled labour than in workers' class solidarity. Unskilled, black and Asian workers were kept out. Its President was Samuel Gompers of the Cigar Makers' union, who had once studied Marxism and rejected it wholly. He argued that labour unions should keep out of politics, but, in fact, threw his weight more than once behind capitalist politicians. When the Republican Senator Mark Hanna formed his Civic Federation within which labour leaders and bosses could collaborate in partnership, Gompers accepted the Vice-Presidency and a $6,000 a year salary. Hanna referred to union leaders like Gompers as the 'labor lieutenants of capital'. De Leon repeated the description as often as he could. Far from wanting to abolish wage labour, Gompers declared that 'The way out of the wage system is through higher wages.'[15] This was not the most promising ground for the SLP to capture.

Lucien Sanial tried to sit as delegate at the AFL convention on behalf of the SLP-dominated Central Labor Federation (CLF). Gompers denied a charter to the CLF because it was affiliated to the SLP and, despite appealing to the Detroit National Convention of the AFL in December 1890, Sanial's credentials as a delegate were denied by 1,699 votes to 535. This still left some base for SLPers within the AFL to work on, and many stayed. In 1893, Thomas J. Morgan of the

Chicago Section of the SLP moved a policy resolution which was put to a referendum of the AFL membership. Of the eleven planks of the Morgan resolution, the most important was Plank Ten, committing the AFL to demand 'the collective ownership by the people of all the means of production and distribution'. The socialists won the vote, but at the Denver National Convention of the AFL in 1894 the Gompers leadership excluded Plank Ten from its programme, inserting instead a vaguely worded opposition to land monopoly. The SLP was strong enough to punish Gompers by ousting him as President, but insufficiently strong to put in a President of their choice. Instead, Gompers was replaced by the miners' leader, John McBride, who was no less corrupt, opportunist and anti-socialist than his predecessor. In 1895 Gompers was re-elected. His first move was to refuse AFL recognition to the New York CLF. Sanial again appealed for the right to sit as a socialist in the AFL. This time he failed and so it was that, in 1895, the SLP entered into official hostility against the AFL.

The Knights of Labor (K of L) was a more appealing setting for socialists, but, by 1891 when De Leon joined it, the movement was becoming a spent force. Formed as a secret Order in 1869, the K of L grew rapidly in the 1880s, when it began to recruit openly. It reached its peak membership in 1886, the momentous year of activity for the eight-hour day: the K of L had over 700,000 members, including the unskilled, unemployed workers and blacks. The Knights were, according to Henry Kuhn, who worked within them. 'quite different from the American Federation of Labor, in organic structure as well as in underlying principle'.[16] He observed that the K of L had 'a distinct revulsion against the craft union spirit' and 'a healthy class instinct'.[17] Engels, a careful observer of the American scene, regarded the K of L as 'a most important factor in the movement which ought not to be pooh-poohed from

41

without but revolutionised from within. . . '.[18]

In July 1891 De Leon, in pursuance of the 'boring from within' policy, was elected to represent New York City local 1563 in District Assembly 49. He soon won the support of the United Hebrew Trades, a union of mainly Jewish Russian *émigrés* working in the New York garment industry, whose political education had been in the fight against Russian autocracy. De Leon won these workers to the cause of socialism and District Assembly 49 became a militant force under the influence of the SLP. This gave De Leon considerable power to determine the future direction of the K of L. The Grand Master Workman (a title remaining from the 'K of L's days as a secret body) was Terence Powderly, whose increasing conservatism was out of tune with the Knights' industrial militancy on the ground. The socialists used their strength in New York to depose Powderly in 1893; as a replacement they gave their support to the Populist-minded James R. Sovereign. De Leon was under no illusion that the new leader would commit the Knights to the revolutionary aim of abolishing the wages system, but he negotiated a deal with Sovereign whereby Sanial would be appointed to edit *The Journal of the Knights of Labour*. De Leon reasoned shrewdly that by attaining socialist control of the union press, the SLP would be able to conduct its propaganda campaign with most success. Having used the socialists to oust Powderly, sovereign proceeded to betray them. Sanial was not offered the editorship as had been agreed. This led De Leon to denounce Sovereign bitterly. At the Washington General Assembly of the K of L during 12–22 November 1895, Sovereign used the union bureaucracy to deny De Leon's credentials as delegate. De Leon fought against this move to oust him and his entire local 1563 from the K of L, but lost the vote narrowly with twenty-one votes for him and twenty-three against. This was the end of 'boring from within' the K of L. De Leon denounced *The Journal of Knights of Labour* as a Populist paper and pulled 13,000 members out of the organisation, leaving it with 17,000 members led by Sovereign, who was to enjoy the unopposed right to preside over its demise.

Alienated from the established trade union movement, De Leon was left in a dilemma. Membership of the AFL and K of L was not worth while from the point of view of using them as forces for socialism, but remaining on the sidelines of the labour unions would place the SLP in sectarian isolation. The chosen way out of the dilemma was to form a new trade union movement based on a recognition of the class struggle and the need to abolish wage slavery. On 6 December 1895 the Socialist Trade and Labor Alliance (STLA) was established. Its formation has been called the most serious tactical error of De Leon's life, so it will be useful to consider the circumstances of its creation.

The vast majority of the American workforce in 1895 was non-unionised; even fifteen years later only 3.7 per cent were in labour unions. Those who were unionised were under the domination of leaders imbued thoroughly with the spirit of class collaboration and craft divisions. Some wits called the AFL the American Separation of Labor because of its defence of specific skills at the expense of class unity. One SLPer, writing to De Leon, referred to his union of window-glass workers as possessing a narrow 'glass consciousness'.[19] No efforts were being made to recruit blacks, women or the unskilled. In the West workers had already rebelled against the old unions and formed their own militant organisations. In 1893 the Western Federation of Miners (WFM) was formed; the same year that Eugene Debs of Terre Haute, Indiana helped to form the American Railway Union (ARU). Both were dual unions, i.e. they were competing for membership with the old, craft trade unions. Both fell out with the AFL's Gompers outlook. Ed

Boyce, the leader of the WFM, wrote to Gompers on 16 March 1897 that 'You know that I am not a trade unionist; I am fully convinced that their day of usefulness is past.'[20] So, contrary to some critics, De Leon and the SLP were not entering into some crazed sectarian scheme when they, too, decided to support dual unionism.

Another criticism made against the formation of the STLA was that it 'came down upon us full-fledged from top to bottom as the masterpiece of our "Master Workman" and took us by surprise'.[21] This claim was made by N. I. Stone in 1899 as an attempt to suggest that the STLA was a product of De Leon's dictatorial whim. In fact, as early as 1889 New York workers were demanding what they called the 'New Trade Unionism'. The city's main union body, the Central Labor Union (CLU), split on this issue and the New Unionists formed the Central Labor Federation (CLF). In December 1889 – before De Leon had joined the SLP – the CLF re-merged with the CLU and was to adopt a constitution calling upon its members not to lend any support 'to the old political parties'. In June 1890 the CLF again split from the CLU because of the latter's decision to support non-socialist candidates in elections, contrary to its constitution. On 3 July 1890 – again, three months before De Leon's arrival on the socialist scene – the CLF resolved:

> That every union affiliating with this Central Labor Federation of New York declares that it is opposed to the existing political parties of capitalism, and favors independent political action by organized labor.[22]

The New York workers' idea spread, first to Brooklyn and Hudson County, New Jersey, and within a short time as far afield as Los Angeles, Wisconsin and Omaha. When the 13,000 members of the K of L, mainly in District Assembly 49, formed the STLA, in 1895, they were not hatching a sectarian scheme, but, after failing to make use of the old unions, they were taking to its practical conclusion the movement initiated in the CLF six years earlier.

At its 1896 National Convention the SLP endorsed the STLA by seventy-one votes to six after an impassioned day-and-a-half debate in which the case for the new union was put by Hugo Vogt. A long resolution was adopted, claiming that 'the AFL and the Knights of Labor . . . have fallen hopelessly into the hands of dishonest and ignorant labor leaders'. Only by recognising that there is a raging class struggle going on could any organisation of labour make progress. Therefore, 'we hail with unqualified joy the formation of the Socialist Trade and Labor Alliance as a giant stride toward throwing off the yoke of wage slavery. . .' 'The revolutionary spirit of the STLA should be taken into all workers' organisations, which would unite into 'one irresistible class-conscious army, equipped both with the shield of the economic organization and the word of the Socialist Labor Party ballot'.[23]

In urging the STLA to take its 'revolutionary spirit' into other organisations, the 1896 resolution appeared to be leaving the door open for socialists still to work within the old unions where expedient. But the SLP did not, in fact, want its members to remain in other bodies. For example, Thomas J. Morgan of Chicago, a dedicated SLPer, had built a solid base within the AFL and refused to leave. Forced to make the choice, Morgan left the SLP.

The 1896 resolution adopted the metaphor of the political sword and the economic shield. This we may call De Leon's early trade union theory. After 1904 he was to reverse the functions of the weapons, seeing the economic movement as the sword and the ballot as the shield (see Chapter 5).

Although only six votes were cast against the SLP's 1896 endorsement of the STLA, and although all of the state

Sections re-endorsed it in their own meetings after the National Convention, the new policy did lead to major unrest in the SLP. Many members viewed the formation of the STLA as a blunder. Some, like Morgan, were genuinely concerned not to alienate decent workers in the rank and file of the old unions. They reasoned that, like it or not, the AFL was where the workers were, and there was no use in socialists abandoning them to complete right-wing control. Other SLPers had less principled opposition to the STLA. They saw the AFL as a source of revenue. For example, the *New Yorker Volkszeitung*, edited by Hermann Schlueter, and the Philadelphia *Tageblatt* – both German-language, SLP paper – could survive only with financial support from AFL-affiliated unions and advertising from capitalist politicians. For men like Schlueter and the lawyer, Morris Hillquit, breaking SLP ties with the AFL was cutting off the hand that fed them.

In 1899, after a failed attempt to take over the SLP, which involved law-suits, punch-ups and heaps of defamation, the *Volkszeitung* faction split from the SLP, taking 2,500 of the 5,000 members. The splitters became known as the 'Kangaroos', a term originally used in the 1850s, when bogus courts had been set up in various south-western states by dubious lawyers who tried people in one area and then leapt off to administer 'justice' elsewhere. Rudolph Katz observed that 'the vast majority of the four hundred sections stood with the party and its duly elected National Executive Committee. Only in comparatively few places did the usurpers, with their secretary, Henry Slobodin, get recognition, endorsement or support'.[24] The 'Kangaroos' did take with them the SLP's German-language paper, the *Volkszeitung*, but before long the Cleveland *Volksfreund* took its place. Out of the split came an intensification of the personal resentment felt by many people towards De Leon. Indeed, it could be argued that the 1899 split was the moment of birth for many of the anti-De Leon sentiments catalogued in Chapter 1. For example, when De Leon stood as a candidate in the 16th District Assembly in 1899, the Kangaroos issued a leaflet stating 'Don't vote for De-Leon [sic]. He is an enemy of Labor, a wrecker of labor organizations, an adventurer, who has done more mischief in workers ranks than any other fiend of organized labor.'[25] Another kangaroo, M. Winchevsky, composed a piece of German doggerel to express his disgust at the narrow principles of De Leon and Hugo Vogt:

Order! Attention!
The Sections must dance
As I strike up the tune for them;
One, two, three and round we go!
Dance, or be ruined
When the boss tells you so

Learn to grasp the need for discipline
Your leader whistles
And You'll know what to do
More and more rigid, more and more narrow
Up with the hand and up with the hammer!
You should be running in rings round me

I will forbid, I can permit
I educate and, if I see fit
Report back to you.
But if you should resist, in the end I'll kill off
the promises, polls and plebiscites,
The 'Pro Forma' you had got

Order! Attention!
The faithful must dance
As I strike up the tune for them

Dance, Germans, Jews and Poles
Just like Daniel told you to,
Just as Hugo orders him.[26]

On 1 January 1900 the Kangaroos held a conference in Rochester, New York and a year and a half later, in Indianapolis, combined with Debs's party, the Social Dem ocratic Party, to form the Socialist Party of America (SPA). From its inception, the SPA was a more popular organisation than the SLP, with a membership of approximately 10,000. Those who formed the SPA did not leave the SLP because De Leon was a tyrant; that was a *post facto* rationalisation. Indeed, they did not leave principally over the issue of dual unionism or because of simply corrupt links with the AFL bureaucracy. They left because De Leon and his party were revolutionaries who sought to abolish the wages system, and they were reformists who would not see beyond the effort to squeeze concessions out of the capitalist system and perhaps one day to manage it.

The formation of the STLA put De Leon outside the main-stream American labour movement. Gompers accused the STLA of union-wrecking; writing to the Alliance's general sec-retary, Ernest Bohn, who had challenged Gompers to debate, the latter responded by complaining that:

> the chief characteristics of your organization since its existence has been to decry the work of the labor movement, to ridicule its accomplishments, to slander the men who have been its staunch-est devotees, only measuring your venom, by the degree of their devotion.[27]

De Leon did not let such comments halt him in his campaign of attack against the 'pure and simple' unions. Their leaders were 'labor lieutenants of capital' and 'fakers', and were obstacles to socialism and therefore such unions must be destroyed.

On 25 November 1900 De Leon went to New Haven, Connecticut to defend in open debate the dual union policy. His opponent was Job Harriman of the Social Democratic Party, which was in 1901, to become the SPA. The contents of this debate reflect well the weaknesses of De Leon's support for dual unionism. De Leon spoke first, and persuasively, in defence of his position. He explained that workers need socialism, but in the meantime required the 'temporary relief' which economic organisation could achieve. The old trade unions, run by class collaborators, were obstacles to such temporary relief; several shocking examples were given of how labour leaders worked with the bosses. It was a waste of time trying to reform such unions: '"Boring from within" resolved itself . . . into this; either you must bore to a purpose, and then you land quickly on the outside, or you knuckle under, a silent supporter of the felonies committed by the labor lieutenants of capitalism.' The STLA was at 'war' with the old unions.[28]

Harriman's response was mainly taken up by a fierce attack upon the STLA's action in one particular strike: that of the Davis Cigar Shop in New York where, it was alleged, the STLA did not recognise the AFL-affiliated International Cigarmakers' union and scabbed on its strike. As one would expect in the case of a heated and destructive inter-union dispute, no one side of the story gave a full picture, and Harriman's claim that De Leon supported scabbing was as false in its incompleteness as Rudolph Katz's subsequent claim, in defence of the STLA, that the Alliance workers had no charges to answer in relation to the Davis incident.[29] The truth is that when two unions regard one another as traitors to the working class, one is quite likely to commit such treachery in its eagerness to destroy the other. The Davis affair certainly damaged the reputation of the STLA and the SLP in New York.

Harriman made another point in his case against the STLA

policy which was very compelling. The old unions, he conceded, did indeed have 'fakers' in them. But even if the majority of trade union leaders were fakers (which Harriman rejected), the majority of the members were honest workers. 'You cannot smash the unions nor stop them from growing', said Harriman. 'They are children of this system, born to stay as long as capitalism stays.'[30] Being 'children of capitalism', their membership will reflect in terms of economic consciousness the level of political consciousness of those they comprise: 'Being composed . . . of precisely the same kind of material as they are now composed of, and the membership being ignorant of the science of Socialism, it is apparent that the unions thus reproduced would be precisely the same as those now in existence. . . .'.[31]) Harriman's logic cannot be faulted here. If, for example, the SLP was 2,000 strong and the STLA 20,000, and if the STLA was not to be corrupt and undemocratic, then 18,000 non-socialists would be able to outvote the 2,000 socialists. If only socialists, capable of joining the SLP, constituted the hypothetical 20,000 members, then why not have 20,000 socialists imposing their might on the existing unions? Or did De Leon propose that by winning the leadership of a union, as the SLP had in the STLA, the majority of its members could be cajoled into class-conscious action? De Leon did not answer the following statement and question which was put to him by Harriman:

> It is a fact that the membership of the unions vote upon the laws that govern them. They also elect their officers by a popular vote. The laws are not made by the officers. I maintain that the wrong laws of the trade union organizations are due, in matters respecting Socialism, to their lack of information and not to their wilful dishonesty. If they are wilfully dishonest, *en masse,* you might as well give up the entire fight, for why should we plead with dishonest men?[32]

In adopting the STLA policy, De Leon was not mistaken in his condemnation of the existing unions. His mistake was to attach too much importance to leadership, assuming that dishonest leaders imposed themselves on unwilling union memberships. The fact was that the Gompers crowd had the support – or, at least, the passive acquiescence – of the workers, and this would not be changed by a retreat into socialist-run unions, but by hard and sustained persuasion of those who accepted the union status quo.

The STLA was never to become a serious force in the industrial struggle. It mainly comprised textile, shoe, metal and engineering workers – never more than 20,000 at the very most. In all, 228 organisations received charters from the STLA, but by 1898 half of these had drifted away, and only half of those remaining paid any dues to the Alliance. The principles of the STLA may have been appealing, but on the economic front unity is strength, and many returned to the fold of the AFL. In 1898 the New York CLF left the STLA over a row about paid advertisements for capitalist politicians in its publication. The STLA's first significant strike action was in June 1899 in Slatersville, Rhode Island. The textile workers involved forced the firm to close, but lost the strike. Another strike, against the Steel Pressed Car company of Pittsburgh, was successful, but most STLA strikes were of little impact.

The STLA struggled on until 1905, when it was to form a movement far bigger and historically more significant than itself: the Industrial Workers of the World (IWW) or 'Wobblies', as they were commonly known. In 1905 the STLA's official membership was 1,450.Contrary to the image of the inflexible dogmatist, De Leon accepted that the STLA policy had been mistaken:

> The Socialist Trade and Labor Alliance was the first labor organization in this country, since the early labor organizations who also

began soundly, that frankly and fully stated to the working class of America that they had to capture the public powers. Their belief is this: That you could not first take the men into the union under the false pretense that you were going to raise their wages, and afterwards indoctrinate them. No, you had to indoctrinate them first, and then bring them in. If the ST & LA has made any mistakes at all, it would be to imagine ten years ago that there were then enough such men in existence to join our ranks.[33]

By the time De Leon made this speech he was part of a new, dynamic, numerically strong union movement, committed to Marx's 'revolutionary watchword, "Abolition of the wages system!"'.[34]

4 The battle against reformism

As the nineteenth-century ended, socialists everywhere were engaged in a process of profound rethinking. They were not entertaining doubts about the need for, and desirability of, the socialist alternative. The growing questioning was about how to achieve the new social order. As the debate proceeded, the participants fell into two camps. One faction doubted the possibility of all-at-once social revolution: change must be piecemeal, chipping away the edifice of the capitalist system only as fast as the possibility for reform would allow. In France these gradualists, under the theoretical guidance of Paul Brousse, became know as the 'possibilists'. The rival camp was given the disparaging label of 'impossibilists'. These were the socialists who saw nothing to be gained, and much to be lost, by compromising with capitalism. The road may be long, the obstacles mighty, the frustration intense, but, reasoned the impossibilists, however hard it is to achieve the socialist transformation of society, any stopping point short of that end is likely to be a diversion. What commenced as a strategic debate amongst comrades developed into undisguised hostility. The possibilists derided the uncompromising zeal of their opponents as dogmatism, fanaticism, political intolerance – indeed, all of the terms which recur tediously in the descriptions of De Leon. The impossibilists, paying little regard to the sincerity of their rivals, portrayed them as mere reformers of capitalism, seeking government office in order to tinker with the effects of the profit system, and all too often to rake off some of the profits for themselves in the process.

Daniel De Leon was the foremost theoretician of impossibilism. Many socialists denied the logic of possibilism; De Leon, more than any other single individual, articulated the theoretical critique of possibilism. Indeed, it was this role which caused De Leon to be so disliked. It would be quite facile to evaluate political thinkers and activists on the basis of their personalities, and it was not because De Leon was a pleasant chap or an unqualified swine that he has been the subject of such passionate depiction. The reality is that impossibilists admired De Leon's sustained analysis of the futility of the possibilist 'something now' approach; while the impossibilist intransigence of this man who refused to trim his demands infuriated the possibilists.

In the USA the SLP was called an impossibilist party by its possibilist rivals in the SPA.[1] The American split between the two tendencies was less clear than in other countries. For example, in France there were the Parti Ouvrier Français and the Fédération des Travailleurs Socialistes de France. The former, led by Jules Guesde and Paul Lafargue, was impossibilist; the latter unreservedly possibilist. In Britain William Morris and other impossibilists broke away from Hyndman's possibilist Social Democratic Federation (SDF) in 1884. In 1903–4 there was an even more explicit 'impossibilist split' away from the SDF. In Bulgaria the impossibilist majority formed what was called the 'Narrow' Socialist Party. In the USA before 1899, the SLP was controlled by impossibilists, although the party maintained a minimum reform programme and had several reformists in its ranks. The breakaway of the 'Kangaroos' left the SLP an overwhelmingly impossibilist party. But the SPA, formed in 1901, was itself divided between a possibilist majority and an impossibilist minority. The latter faction had the passive backing of the party's leading figure, Eugene Debs, who referred to the possibilist majority as the 'Slowcialists'. In short, impossibilism was of greater significance in the socialist movement of the USA than it tended to be in Europe.

What was De Leon's attitude to reforms? He welcomed any concessions which the profit system might offer, but 'while not opposing any reforms or improvements which may be secured under capitalism, the Socialist Labor Party steadfastly sets its face against taking time away from its main battle, for revolution, in order to carry on the struggle for reform'.[2] Five years after joining the SLP, De Leon formulated his position on reforms in his address, 'Reform or Revolution', in which the terms are defined: 'Reform means a change of externals; revolution – peaceful or bloody, the peacefulness of bloodiness of it cuts no figure whatever in the essence of the question – means a change from within.'[3] Three main objections to reformism, or the struggle for 'immediate demands' from capitalist governments, were put by De Leon at different times. The first was that reform is a sop to put off revolution: when a ruling class is under threat of resistance from the ruled it throws crumbs at them in order to preserve its possession of the whole cake. On 2 and 16 April 1902, De Leon gave two speeches: 'Plebs Leaders and Labor Leaders'; and 'The Warning of the Gracchi'. These were published together under the title *Two Pages From Roman History*. Citing detailed references to the trickery used by the Roman rulers to maintain the plebeians in subjection, De Leon showed how the modern capitalist rulers use similar methods – such as buying off the workers' leaders and offering limited concessions so as to bribe the wage slaves into passivity:

> Request a little, when you have a right to the whole, and your request, whatever declamatory rhetoric or abstract scientific verbiage it be accompanied with, works a subscription to the principle that wrongs you . . . The palliative, accordingly, ever steels the wrong that is palliationed.[4]

55

De Leon's second objection to reforms was that, whereas the revolutionary is quite happy to see capitalism improved for the workers while working as a socialist for revolution, the reformist is not happy to contemplate revolution but confines himself solely to schemes for running capitalism.

In an editorial in the *Daily People* on 15 June 1909, De Leon asks:

> What is 'reform'? For that we must go to the reformer himself. He is perfectly explicit in what he is not. The reformer firmly objects to revolution. He holds the thing to be harmful in theory, still more harmful in practice . . . He holds tenaciously to the essence of what is . . . Without upsetting the essence, the reformer seeks to improve details.

In this way it is the possibilist who is depicted as the dogmatist, rather than the revolutionary. And why not? There are no more grounds historically for the belief that nothing can be achieved except within capitalism than for the rival dogma that absolutely nothing is achievable until capitalism is destroyed. De Leon did not adhere to this latter belief: he understood that trade unions can obtain economic gain and that certain kinds of political reforms, discussed below, could improve capitalism. The main point of the second objection, however, was that reformists want to leave the reformed system intact.

The third objection to reformism was that reformed capitalism will be presented as socialism. De Leon insisted that:

> socialism means but one thing, and that is the abolition of capital in private hands, and the turning over of the industries into the direct control of the workmen employed in them. Anything else is not socialism, and has no right to sail under that name. Socialism is not the establishment of an eight-hour day, not the abolition of child labor, not the enforcement of pure food laws, not the putting down of the Night Riders, or the enforcement of the 80-cent gas law. None of these, nor all of them together, are

socialism. They might all be done by the government tomorrow, and still we would not have socialism. They are merely reforms on the present system, mere patches on the worn-out garment of industrial servitude, and are no more socialism than the steam from a locomotive is the locomotive.[5]

In saying that legislation for the eight-hour day or the abolition of child labor is not socialism, De Leon was not saying that these reforms would not be welcomed by socialists. The point is that even if these reforms of capitalism were brought about – as, of course, they have been – the socialist alternative will still be as necessary as it was before. If, however, such reforms were advocated by socialists, and if it suited the capitalists to concede them, then it would appear that socialism had somehow been provided, or partially established. Socialism is not a gift to be provided by capitalist governments, and De Leon feared that reorganised capitalism could be used to divert workers' attention from the real alternative.

When De Leon spoke of 'reforms', he tended to mean economic palliatives. These were not worth advocating for the reasons given. A distinction was made, however, between such economic tinkering with the system and political reforms, i.e. those which, if passed, would change the Constitution so as to make for a more democratic atmosphere in which to work for socialism. For example, De Leon argued forcefully in the *Daily People* for the principle of recall. A correspondent to De Leon's 'Letter Box' column asked: 'Is the recall to be considered a reform? If so, is not your plan for the recall at variance with the general attitude of your party towards reforms?' De Leon replied by stating that 'The recall is not a reform – at least not a reform in the category that the Socialist Labor Party warns against. The reforms that the SLP warns against are nonpolitical and economic in their nature.'[6]

Again, in 1910, Victor Berger of the SPA was elected to

57

Congress as Representative for the Fifth Congress District of the State of Wisconsin. De Leon was merciless in his relentless criticism of the behaviour of this 'first Socialist in Congress'. He wrote a series of articles between April and October 1911 (published by the SLP as a pamphlet entitled *A Socialist in Congress – His Conduct and Responsibilities*, in which he carefully detailed the 'hits' and 'misses' of Berger's career in Congress. Thirty 'misses' were dealt with, but, in his article of 14 May 1911, De Leon wrote of 'Berger's Hit No. 1'. This was because Berger moved an amendment to the American Constitution empowering a majority of members of Congress to call for the setting up of a national convention to change the Constitution. In the midst of De Leon's campaign of attack upon Berger's reformist position, De Leon pauses in the case of this one proposed political reform and states that 'we gladly credit him with the purpose of intentionally rendering the Constitution more readily responsive to the progressive sentiments of our people'.[7]

Another political reform to which De Leon attached great importance was women's suffrage. During his lifetime American women did not have the vote, except in the four states of Colorado, Utah, Idaho and Wyoming. In 1904 the NYLN published De Leon's translation of Bebel's *Woman Under Socialism*. In his Translator's Preface, De Leon stated that 'the invocation of the "Rights of Woman" . . . rouses the spirit of the heaviest sufferers under capitalist society . . .'[8] On 8 May 1909 De Leon spoke in New York under the title of 'Woman Suffrage'. While opposing the arguments often put by suffragettes, who offered pleas to the capitalist rulers on the basis of all kinds of spurious claims, such as that women invented industry or can save civilisation or are entitled to 'justice', De Leon committed himself to women's suffrage. To the opponents of such reform who claimed that women are not fit to make political decisions, De Leon responded that that was:

exactly what they say of the working class – exactly the language of King George and his Parliament toward the American colonists in revolt . . . In short, exactly the language that usurpation ever holds, and that regularly is disproved, as soon as its yoke is cast off.[9]

In opposition to racism De Leon was just as vociferous. At the Amsterdam Congress of the Second International, which he attended in 1904, he spoke in vigorous opposition to immigration controls, advocated by delegates from the SPA. Unlike the SLP, the SPA's record on racism was atrocious. At its 1908 National Convention one of its leaders, Ernest Untermann, stated that 'I am determined that my race shall be supreme in this country and in the world.'[10] The SPA delegation in Amsterdam advocated immigration restriction against what they called 'backward races . . . such as Chinese, Negroes etc.' In Texas as well as some other states the SPA had segregated Sections for Negroes. This infuriated De Leon:

Why should a truly Socialist organization of whites not take in Negro members, but organize these in separate bodies? On account of outside prejudice? Then the body is not truly Socialist. A Socialist body that will trim its sails . . . to 'outside prejudices' had better quit. A truly Socialist body is nothing if not a sort of 'Rough on Prejudices' . . . Ten to one, however, where the 'issue' arises in such a body it is catering, not to outside, but to inside prejudices, to the prejudices of the members themselves.[11]

De Leon opposed not only racism but also its imperialist cause. In 1898, when the Spanish–American war was declared, De Leon wrote to the workers of the Spanish Empire that 'across the smoke of belching cannons, and the flood of human gore that this war will cause to flow, we, the class conscious proletariat of America reach you the hand of brotherhood. . .'[12]

So it would be a mistake to regard De Leon's refusal to join the struggle for economic reform as an indication that he

59

opposed economic improvements, or opposed all reforms, or that he remained detached from day-to-day issues, such as war, racism and sexism.

When De Leon joined the SLP in 1890 it had yet to clarify its position regarding alliances with non-revolutionary organisations. Having been used and rebuffed by the United Labor Party in 1886, the SLP was disinclined to enter into further coalitions. In the 1890s Populism emerged as a powerful agrarian force. The Populists did not adopt Marxist theory or appeal to the lot of the industrial worker, but were based upon a spontaneous revulsion by small farmers and non-urban workers against the alienation and poverty which were the the hallmarks of the 'gilded age'. The Populists appealed to the man 'who labors hard from fourteen to sixteen hours a day to obtain the bare necessaries of life'. And they asked, as did the Populist newspaper in Lincoln, Nebraska, the *Farmers' Alliance*, 'How can you reach this man, how kindle the divine spark which is torpid in his soul, when he knows that it is greed that enforces the material labor that is crushing him down, when he feels it is the wage system that is stealing the fruits of his toil and abasing and enslaving him?'[13] Much of what the Populists said was close to the SLP message and this did not escape De Leon. In De Leon's first three years in the SLP some Sections worked officially or otherwise in unison with the Populists. In 1893 the SLP Constitution was amended so as to prevent such coalition; this led to a few Sections leaving, but the majority accepted the need for opposition to the possibilists of the Populist Movement, recognising them as a reformist force. As the historian of Populist ideas, Norman Pollack, has pointed out, 'Perhaps Henry D. Lloyd best expressed the relation of Populism and Socialism', when he wrote to the president of Iowa College that he would not associate with the SLP, but 'if I were in England I should certainly have affiliated with the

Fabian Society'.[14] The Populists' 'exemplificaton of pure social-ism' in the USA was 'our public school system and our postal system'.[15] Clearly, a gulf divided such thinking from the revolu-tionary SLP. In 'Reform or Revolution' De Leon dismissed Populism as a 'false movement' which 'proceeded upon lines of ignorance'[16] 'If bluff and blarney could save a movement', stat-ed De Leon, 'the People's Party would have been imperish-able.'[17]

In its hostile response to Populism the SLP opened itself up to the accusation of sectarianism. 'I am a Populist,' wrote John Jones Smith to the *Weekly People* of 6 September 1895, 'and can't agree with you Socialists in all your demands. I think you want too much all at once.' This was classical possibilism, but it could be argued that by working alongside men such as John Jones Smith the principles of socialism could have obtained at least a hearing in such quarters. In the same year another Populist, B. F. Fries, wrote to inform the SLP of the effect of its persistent criticism of the People's Party:

> Our P. P. Club here are almost to a man 'out-and-out" Socialists in principle, and yet I am sorry to tell you this fact: that a year ago, at every meeting, the reading of *The People* was warmly applauded, now it is coldly received.[18]

Again, in 1895, an unsigned letter to the *People* stated that 'At present I favour the Populist Party, and I am sorry to see you lecturing the infant class for stupidity, because they are just beginning to learn how much they have to learn.'[19]

In mid-1896 the St Louis Convention of the People's Party voted for electoral fusion with the Democratic Party, with William Jennings Bryan appointed as Presidential Candidate. This fusion split the Populists, who declined as a political force after that. Some of them turned to the SLP, seeing it as the truly radical third political force which they had wanted the

People's Party to be. M. W. Wilkins wrote to Kuhn on 19 June 1896 that, 'In common with a vast number of people I thought that the People's Party was travelling toward the Cooperative Commonwealth. Events sometimes open ones eyes wide and quick. The St Louis Convention to which I was a delegate performed that office for me . . . I learned that all the leaders desired nothing more than to 'reform' (patch up) the present system.'[20]

By the late 1890s the SLP's policy was fundamentally anti-possibilist. Its membership was not overwhelmingly of that outlook. The 1899 split was not essentially about specific SLP policies, but was a final effort by approximately half of its members to assert the compatibility between a socialist party and a possibilist strategy or, conversely, to remove what they saw as the theoretical shackles of De Leon's uncompromising impossibilism. The possibilists who gathered around the *New Yorker Volkszeitung* looked to the European social-democratic parties as their model, particularly the German SPD. European 'socialists' all advocated minimum, immediate demand programmes as well as maximum demands for complete socialist transformation. By the late 1890s the European parties had come to place little emphasis upon the maximum aim of displacing capitalism and became increasingly immersed in the established trade unions and schemes for welfare reform. It is no coincidence that the year of the split saw the publication of Edward Bernstein's *Evolutionary Socialism*, which constituted the most fundamental revision of Marxist theory in the light of the European social-democratic experience. The *Volkszeitung* faction sought to bring the SLP into line with the European possibilists. This theory of the split was not articulated by De Leon; he did not speak in terms of possibilism versus impossibilism. De Leon saw the split as being specifically rooted in the trade union policy of the SLP, as he wrote in an article on 'The

Socialist Movement in America' in the 1908 Almanac of the SLP Hungarian journal, *Nepakarat*:

> The ST & LA was no sooner launched than it became the bitter target for the assault of the AF of L. The struggle was, of course, carried into the Party by the representatives of the AF of L, and a conflict ensued that culminated in a split in 1899. One portion of the SLP pulled out and declared 'neutrality' toward unionism, while the body of the SLP pronounced 'neutrality' only a mast behind which to conceal partisanism in favor of corrupt unionism.[21]

Arnold Petersen, who dominated the SLP for many years after De Leon's death, saw the 1899 split as a result of the 1890 'break with the old reform strivings', which dominated the SLP before De Leon's entry, not being clean or sharp enough. The pre-De Leon SLP's reformism haunted the post-1890 party:

> and before long the SLP found itself divided into two main hostile factions – the Marxist Wing headed by De Leon, Henry Kuhn, Sanial and others; and the reform and craft union element led by Abraham Cahan of the Jewish *Forward*, Morris Hillquit, the ambitious and client-hungry lawyer, the *Volkszeitung* crowd, and others of their ilk.[22]

The failure of the July 1899 attempt to oust De Leon from his position of political eminence in the party and to wrest control of the *People*, in order to turn it into a pro-reform newspaper linked to the old unions, signalled the total defeat of SLP possibilism. With the removal of the Kangaroos, the ideological authority of De Leon was unchallenged and the move to all-out impossibilism was unimpeded.

From 2 to 8 June 1900 at the Grand Central Palace, New York City, the Tenth National convention of the SLP assembled. The Ninth Convention – which was, in fact, the first SLP

63

Convention to include delegates from beyond New York – had met in 1896 and had endorsed the STLA. The Tenth Convention was attended by delegates from the following states: California (one delegate), Connecticut (four), Illinois (one), Indiana (one), Kentucky (one), Maryland (one), Massachusetts (eleven), Michigan (one), Minnesota (one), Missouri (one), New Jersey (seven), New York (thirty-one), Ohio (four), Pennsylvania (eleven), Rhode Island (four), Washington (one), Wisconsin (one) and Virginia (one). The delegates listened to a detailed (twenty-five page) report from Henry Kuhn, the National Secretary, in which the Kangaroos were portrayed as devious conspirators and anti-socialists without principles. That the possibilists had been removed from the ranks was regarded as a gain in the party's strength, even though it had halved the membership. For, as De Leon had advised the socialists of Boston in 1896:

> No organization will inspire the outside masses with respect that will not insist upon and enforce discipline within its own ranks. If you allow your own members to play monkeyshines with the party, the lookers-on . . . will justly believe that you will at some critical moment allow capitalism to play monkeyshines with you; they will not respect you, and their accession to your ranks will be delayed.[23]

It is only within the context of that perspective that one can comprehend the high morale which characterised the 1900 Convention.

The Convention was explicitly conscious of its task of completing the break with possibilism. Thomas Curran, the temporary chairman for the first day, set off the Convention as it was to proceed:

> The Socialist Labor Party, starting out in this year 1900, no doubt will take a position that will leave it clear before . . . the wage-

workers of the country as to what it proposes to accomplish and what means it proposes to employ to accomplish its ends. With other parties posing before the people as Socialist parties, with the so-called 'respectable' party – the Social Democratic Party – and with that other mongrel now known as the 'Kangaroos', it is fitting and time for the genuine, *bona fide*, proletarian, Socialist Movement as represented by the Socialist Labor Party, to be laid before the proletarians of the country in as uncompromising and clearcut a manner as is possible. The time is past when we can stop and consider the objection of this and that freak who happened to belong to us . We have now come to the time when we must cut our lines clear and sharp and push out those who do not belong to us.[24]

It was as if a new party were being formed, based upon the purity of the De Leon position. Like Curran, De leon spoke on the first day about the immense changes in the party; the SLP 'of 1900', he said, 'is not simply four years older than it was four years ago; it is fully forty years older'. 'Never before has a National Convention . . . met under circumstances so auspicious as those that attend this national gathering . . .' proclaimed Kuhn.[25]

Aside from the self-important rhetoric, the 1900 Convention did accomplish three significant changes to the SLP, completing its evolution as a thoroughly De Leonist party. First, party discipline was tightened and made more centralised; secondly, the SLP broke all links with the 'pure and simple' trade unions; and thirdly, the minimum programme of 'immediate demands' was dropped.

A series of constitutional amendments was carried by the Convention which concentrated its power in the New York-based National Executive Committee (NEC). Centralisation did not amount to increased power for De Leon; in fact, he was not an NEC member and, as a (theoretically) salaried editor of

65

the *People*, the revised Constitution forbade him from standing for election to the NEC. In future, only the NEC could authorise the publication of SLP literature. This was a direct response to the *Volkszeitung* experience, in which legal control of the newspaper was in the hands of the non-party controlled Socialist Cooperative Publishing Company. The revised Constitution created a swifter mechanism for expelling members thought to be disrupters. In many respects the SLP prefigured the centralised and disciplined structure to be established three years later in the Russian Bolshevik Party.

The 1896 National Convention had endorsed the STLA but had remained ambiguous about members' right to stay within the 'pure and simple' unions. The 1900 Convention carried an amendment to its Constitution, moved by delegates Meiko Meyer of Michigan and Daniel De Leon of New York, stating that:

> If any member of the Socialist Labor Party accepts office in a pure and simple labor organization, he shall be considered antagonistically inclined towards the Socialist Labor Party and shall be expelled. If any officer of a pure and simple trade or labor organization applies for membership in the Socialist Labor Party, he shall be rejected.[26]

This change was not accepted without heated debate. Kuhn could not accept it; his knowledge of the SLP nationally convinced him that many principled, militant SLPers were working hard in the old unions. Often they had little choice, for the STLA was far from being a national movement. That socialists held union offices was seen as a base from which to convince union members of the validity of socialist principles. If socialists could not retain elected office in unions they would merely be handing them over to reactionary leaders. De Leon reasoned that 'pure and simple' unions belonged to the 'fakers' and that socialists should let them take office. Furthermore, De Leon told the Convention that STLA members should not be allowed to be politically active except in the SLP. De Leon's position – and that adopted by the 1900 Convention – was hopelessly misinformed about the condition of American trade unionism. De Leon believed that 'pure and simpledom' was on the decline and the STLA principle was on the upsurge. The reverse was the real situation: the AFL was growing and the STLA shrinking into an economically impotent appendage of the SLP. In 1896 the party had been urged to endorse the STLA in an effort to provide a militant union base for those who could no longer work within the AFL. Now, those who could work within the AFL – or even non-AFL affiliated, non-STLA unions – were being denied the right to do so in any official capacity. Looking back on the decision in 1919, by which time the SLP had abandoned the prohibition in question, Kuhn commented that the SLP 'had drawn the bow too tight', but, by the time it realised its error, 'the damage had been done and could not easily be repaired'.[27] Kuhn recalled that this was the first issue of importance on which he had not been persuaded by De Leon.

By far the most important decision of the 1900 Convention was taken on the morning of the fourth day. Like all nineteenth-century Marxist parties, the SLP had a minimum as well as a maximum programme. The 1896 Convention had adopted a platform beginning with the declaration of its maximum aim:

> the abolition of classes, the restoration of the land and all the means of production, transportation and distribution to the people as a collective body, and the substitution of the Co-operative Commonwealth for the present state of planless production, industrial war and social disorder; a Commonwealth in which every worker shall have the free exercise and full benefit of his faculties, multiplied by all the modern factors of civilization.[28]

There then followed a list of reform proposals presented 'with a view to immediate improvement in the condition of labour'.

The twenty-one immediate demands ranged from a call for the United States to have exclusive right to issue money', to 'progressive income tax and tax on inheritance', to 'Equalization of woman's wages with those of men where equal service is performed'. Those who had split in 1899 were seen by De Leon as placing excessive emphasis on the reform programme. They were seeking votes to amend and not to end the capitalist system.

This explains why Lucien Sanial, speaking on behalf of the Committee on Platform and Resolutions (comprising himself, Eberle of Pennsylvania, Dalton of Washington, Hickey of New York and and De Leon) recommended:

> that the platform of the Socialist Labor Party . . . be readopted word for word and the whole string of planks, that remind us of the infancy of Socialists, when Socialists were still impressed with the idea that we must do something immediately for the working class . . . be stricken out and the Declaration of Principles alone remain.[29]

Delegates were virtually unanimous in their support for dropping the 'immediate demands'. Paul Dinger of Ohio expressed the view that the minimum programme confused those hearing the socialist argument: 'Those of us who have had experience on the stump know very well that those "planks" stood in our way. They tended to confuse audiences; they gave a way to the capitalists and their agents and other quibblers to show that the Socialist Labor Party . . . advocated municipal ownership of industries . . .'[30] Thomas Curran's view was that the 'immediate demands' were useful as 'baits' to workers in times past, but now the SLP had reached the point where it could appeal to those who wanted 'Socialism pure and simple' and 'we can now afford to leave to the freak elements, the Populist Party, the Debs Party, and the Kangaroo Party, all these demands that tie us down to present conditions and make us almost part of them'.[31] Boris Reinstein, a New York delegate, explained that he used to think it neces- sary 'to have a program maximum and a program minimum so as to build up the Party'. In short, the reform 'planks' had been conceived as an opportunist means of party-building, like that employed by the European social-democrats. Reinstein's analysis was that much as a reform programme did attract members, it inevitably recruited reformists, who joined the SLP or voted for it for the wrong reasons. Thus, Reinstein argued, by deleting the minimum programme, the party's membership would undergo a process of 'natural selection', whereby those remaining 'will be attracted by its main, revolu- tionary spirit, and not by any compromising considerations . . .'[32] De Leon was utterly convinced of the need to drop the minimum programme:

> It is the navel string that connected the active fighting SLP with the embryo SLP at a time when we had to go around with our hats in our hands, and try to sugar-coat our principles, and show people what we might do. And it was very dangerous, because, by telling people what we might do – all of which things did not in any way affect the fundamental thing that we were after, name- ly, the abolition of the wages system – we simply notified the freaks and capitalists through what doors they could get into our citadel and knock us out.[33]

The decision to delete the minimum programme was carried by seventy-two votes to two. It was the most important deci- sion ever to be made at an SLP Convention. Committed solely to the maximum demand of abolishing the wages system not in a piecemeal fashion but with a single revolutionary blow, the SLP converted itself into a thoroughly impossibilist party. It was not alone in this position. From France, where the possi- bilists and impossibilists had split eighteen years before the Tenth Convention of the SLP, the Parti Ouvrier Français sent a resolution to the assembled SLPers, asserting its 'entire solidarity of socialist conception and tactics with the Comrades of the Socialist Labor Party, working like they do, upon the sole ground of the class struggle for the overthrow of the capitalist system'.[34] The SLP reciprocated with a resolution expressing its solidarity with the French impossibilists.

France was the centre of the possibilist–impossibilist conflict which dominated the international socialist movement in the year 1900. The Second International had been established eleven years earlier, marking the centenary of the French revolution. At the inception of the Second International the French possibilists had convened a rival international Congress, to be free from Marxist influence. The possibilist International came to nothing, and so it was that the Second International was a loose coalition between Marxist revolutionaries and social-democratic reformists. In 1889 the SLP sent two delegates (J. F. Busche and J. Miller) to the founding Congress of the International; they did not attend the possibilist Congress, although the SLP at that time had voted to attend both. In 1891 Sanial represented the SLP in Brussels, and in 1893 De Leon attended his first International Congress, in Zurich, accompanied by Sanial, who went as delegate for the CLF. At the 1896 London Congress Matthew Maguire was delegate for the SLP, with Sanial on this occasion representing the STLA.

The 1900 Congress was in Paris. The SLP was represented by six delegates, including Sanial. The pressing problem of the Congress concerned the dilemma about Millerandism. In 1899 Alexandre Millerand, a French possibilist socialist, had been given a job as Minister of Commerce by the Waldeck–Rousseau government. Not only did Millerand accept this highly capitalist post in an openly bourgeois government, but, as if to add insult to injury in the eyes of revolutionary socialists, he sat in the cabinet with Gallifet, the notorious butcher of the Paris Commune. The question before the Paris Congress was: should socialists take office in capitalist governments? Two resolutions reflected the rival camps. The French impossibilist, Jules Guesde, proposed that socialists should only take administrative power when elected on the basis of a principled policy. Karl Kautsky's alternative resolution was crammed full of reluctant sentiments about socialist membership of capitalist governments, but concluded that such participation is acceptable unless 'the government gives evidences of partiality in the struggle between capital and labour'. The SLP delegates contended that no capitalist government ever had been, nor ever could be, impartial in the class struggle. The Kautsky resolution obtained twenty-four votes in the committee set up to formulate a policy on Millerandism. Only four votes were cast for the Guesde resolution: by Guesde, on behalf of the Parti Ouvrier Français; by Enrico Ferri, for the Italian Left; by the Bulgarian 'Narrows'; and by the SLP.

At the 1904 Amsterdam Congress, De Leon represented the SLP, together with Moritz Poehland. Why did De Leon participate in the predominantly possibilist Second International? 'Despite all seeming wranglings, sometimes even wars, among them, the capitalist class is international, and presents a united front against the working class. But for that very reason the capitalist class is interested in keeping the workingmen divided among themselves.'[35] If it is in the capitalists' interest to have working-class disunity, then, reasoned De Leon, socialists must promote international working-class unity, even if, as was the case after 1900, it meant that the SLP had to sit as a minority of the American delegation alongside the SPA at the International Congresses.

Whilst participating in the International, De Leon evolved his own theory of European reformism. Unlike the fully developed capitalist republics such as the USA and France, the majority of

71

the European nations were regarded by De Leon as being semi-feudal. In line with his view that political–democratic reforms, as opposed to economic palliatives, were worth supporting, De Leon came to think that the overwhelmingly reform-centered programmes of the European socialist parties, notably the German SPD, were justified. In short, European possibilism was tolerable because of the material backwardness of countries like Germany and Britain. This was a revised outlook for De Leon; in the 1890s he had looked to the European socialists as the carriers of deeper experience and more sophisticated principles than the infant Marxists of the USA. By 1904 De Leon felt able to explain the possibilist character of the European social-democrats:

> Seeing that that which it opposes, or confronts, is not capitalism in its purity, but feudalism soused with capitalism – as surviving feudal institutions are bound to be at this late date – the party of Bebel has by the force of circumstances been constrained to take the leadership and become the embodiment of radical bourgeois reforms.[36]

So, possibilism is justifiable when reforms are possible and where that is the case:

> they are so just because a true Socialist Movement is not yet possible – a feudal class, still mighty, though crowded by its upstart rival, the capitalist, and just because of being thus crowded, will lend a helping hand to what instinctively it feels to be its rising rival's predestined slayer. SO LONG AS SUCH REFORMS ARE TO BE GAINED, THEY SHOULD BE STRIVEN FOR.[37]

It was in this context that De Leon attended the Amsterdam Congress in 1904. His principal task was to rescind the theoretically unsound Kautsky resolution. His own resolution reflected his theory of American and French exceptionalism. It called for the repeal of the Kautsky resolution 'as a principle of general Socialist tactics'. He conceded that the resolution could have some European application 'perhaps, in countries not yet wholly freed from feudal institutions', but he utterly repudiated Kautsky's non-Marxist thinking about the neutrality of the state and asserted that 'in fully developed capitalist countries like America, the working class cannot, without betrayal of the cause of the proletariat, fill any political office other than they conquer for and by themselves'.[38] De Leon was the sole voter for his own motion on the International Bureau. Finally, the Dresden resolution, disowning the Kautsky position and condemning what it called 'revisionist tactics', was carried by twenty-seven votes to three, with De Leon voting for. Despite his reputation as an inflexible and undiplomatic purist, De Leon did cast his vote for a resolution which he considered less satisfactory than his own, on the pragmatic ground that 'there was nothing for me to do but to vote for the Dresden resolution as the best thing that could be obtained under the circumstances'.[39]

When he returned from the Congress, De Leon compiled his *Flashlights of the Amsterdam Congress*, a work of unique impossibilist insight into the ideas and personalities of the Second International. Jean Jaurès, the French apologist for Miller-andism is described as a utopian socialist: 'an unqualified nuisance in the Socialist Movement of the world at large, of France in particular. He must be removed – with all the tenderness that is possible, but with all the harshness that may be necessary'.[40] In contradistinction, Guesde, as the leading French impossibilist, he saw as 'the most pregnant' of 'the many notabilities in the Socialist Movement of the Continent'.[41] Other sketches are masterstrokes of political impressionism: the Austrian, Victor Adler is depicted as an equivocating philosopher: 'As absurd as the revolutionist would be in a seance of philosophers, so absurd is the philosopher in a council of war. The former is a

73

bull in a china-shop, the latter a mill-stone around the neck. I mean neither to flatter nor insult when I say that Adler is a Montaigne out of season.'[42] Van Koll, the leader of the Dutch delegation, who moved a racist anti-immigration resolution, is described as 'dull and bovine. His face had no more expression while he spoke than a pitcher of water when the water is flowing out'.[43]

In the Second International one sees a different side of De Leon: tolerant of impure actions, willing to compromise where he could achieve most of what he wanted, observing his European comrades with a resigned attitude which was almost condescension. Kretlow, who was SLP delegate at the 1900 Congress, went even further than De Leon in his contempt for the so-called great socialist leaders of Europe. He commented that, 'I will say that I have met men here who were considered socialists and were delegates that we in the States would take by the slack of the pants and kick through the door.'[44] No such sentiments were exhibited by De Leon back in the USA against his reformist foe of the SPA. At the Amsterdam Congress, and at the Congresses at Stuttgart in 1907 and Copenhagen in 1910, where De Leon also represented the SLP, unity resolutions were carried which called upon rival socialist parties existing in countries represented at the International to fuse. De Leon and the SPA delegates overtly supported these calls for unity, each blaming the other for blocking fusion. The reality was that De Leon could not operate inside a non-impossibilist party like the SPA. The SPA debated fusion with the SLP at its 1908 Convention, but could not for one moment entertain the idea of incorporating the De Leon line. The fact was that both parties denied the socialist credentials of the other. In 1909 the SPA attempted to oust De Leon from his place on the International Socialist Bureau; Morris Hillquit argued that the SLP was practically dead, only De

Leon remained and the SPA should be the sole representative of the American socialists as it had 53,375 members. This led the Polish Marxist, Rosa Luxemburg, successfully to oppose the move by stating that 'The leading feature of Hillquit's speech is an inextricable contradiction to me. I do not understand how, if the SP is as large as it claims and the SLP consists of De Leon only, one single man could so tremendously hurt 53,375 others.'[45]

De Leon was under no illusion that the Second International was a force for socialism. He did think that, at best, it could serve as an anti-war council of the European working class. Even in this slight hope, De Leon's optimism had the better of him. In 1914, the year of De Leon's death, the Second International collapsed as all of the European possibilists rushed to support their rival masters in the imperialist world war: Millerand became French Minister of War in 1915 and President of the Third Republic in 1924. De Leon's fear about 'socialists' joining capitalist governments were proved to have been quite right.

In the USA socialists were not faced with the problem of being asked to serve in government as a result of their electoral strength. The votes received by the SLP were insignificantly small. Despite the hopes of the 1900 Convention that a new age of principled campaigning in elections would bring greater victories for the SLP, the fact was that the party's 1898 national poll was the highest it was ever to receive. In 1900 the SLP vote was less than half of what is had been two years earlier, and by 1908 it was less than a quarter. In 1894 Matthew Maguire had been elected as an SLP alderman in Paterson, New Jersey, and shortly afterwards John H. Connor was elected to local office in Holyoke, Massachusetts. Such victories did not motivate the capitalist political leaders to rush to De Leon's office to negotiate terms of socialist entry into the Administration.

The SPA did much better electorally, both in its Debs Presidential campaigns and in winning widespread municipal representation. The election of Berger as 'the first Socialist in Congress' was seen by De Leon as a victory for unprincipled reformism and, in so far as Berger could have used Congress as a propaganda platform, an entirely missed opportunity. When Berger made his maiden speech, De Leon noted with anger that it contained no 'argument to enable the wage-slave class to bowl down the preachments of the pack of politicians, professors and pulpiteers, along with their capitalist press, whose function is to fill the air with false and conflicting and confusing reasoning'.[46] In July, 1911, Berger proposed a bill to provide old age pensions. For De Leon, here was a case study of the hopeless limitations of economic reform. First, the pension could be claimed only by workers over the age of sixty, but, pointed out De Leon, 'the average life of the American soldier of industry is barely 40 . . .' Secondly, convicted felons, including workers found guilty of crimes conducted in the trade union struggle, were disqualified from receiving the pension. Thirdly, workers with a weekly income of $6 would receive no pension. Fourthly, the orphans of workers sent to early graves 'on the firing line of industry' would receive no pensions. And, finally, the pension proposed by Berger to those who have put in 'Sixty years of toil and poverty that yielded affluence into the coffers of the Capitalist Class' would be, on average, $1.50 a week.[47]

For De Leon, the half decade after the 1900 Convention were years of bitter frustration. Workers did not flock to the impossibilist principles of the SLP; in fact, support dropped. From the party's new premises at 2–6 New Reade Street, in the City Hall area of New York City, De Leon presided in the small, third-floor office as editor of a daily newspaper which, as Kuhn had warned, was placing an impossible strain on the few activitists of the SLP. Within a few years of the 1899 split more internal dissension emerged. In the years 1901 and 1902 the SLP lost nearly all of its major personalities, with the exception of De Leon. The entire Pennsylvania State Executive Committee resigned in a row over the location of NEC. Julian Pierce, the head of the NYLN went; so did T. A. Hickey, a paid speaker for the party; Curran, Keinard and Keep left; Sanial resigned; and even Hugo Vogt, the comrade of whom 'De Leon often said that no man was ever so near and dear to him', went out.[48] Rudolph Katz recalled how so many 'functionaries of the party, agitators, organizers, members of the editorial staff of the *Daily People*, secretaries of state committees, writers in prose and writers in rhyme – all went helterskelter down the incline from the heights occupied by the Socialist Labor Party' that 'De Leon remarked that he had to look at himself in the mirror at least once a day to find out whether he had not gone with the others!' Katz's explanation of the exodus is probably as good as any:

> Some got tired when they realized that the onward march of the revolutionary Socialist Labor Party would not be a succession of brilliant dashes carrying with it all the glory of the day. Others saw a very meager opportunity for a meager life; some were made to think that the Socialist Labor Party was doomed, and still others of the rank and file were misled, the majority of whom however, realizing their mistake, came back again into the folds of the party.[49]

These were, indeed, dark years for Danial De Leon. His political obituary was being written as his party crumbled to pieces, and he must have suspected the validity of some of the rumours of his own demise as an influence upon the American socialist movement. Interestingly, De Leon faced many of these traumas miles away from New York, at the country summer retreat in Milford, Connecticut which Bertha persuaded him to rent. There De Leon swam and fished for clams, writing his pieces for the *Daily People*, and maintaining correspondence with Kuhn and others on an old wooden kitchen table which he used as a desk. With his children and wife De Leon could escape from the image of himself which was regularly brought out in order to beat the SLP. He could be himself: a husband and father, a revolutionary socialist and irrepressible impossibilist.

5 De Leon and the Wobblies

As the year 1904 passed away, De Leon, less than a month into his fifty-second year, had strong reason to feel demoralised. The gallery of enemies poised in opposition to him, many of them close comrades of recent years, was enough to make any man feel out in the cold. The SLP was declining in size and electoral support; the STLA, with a membership of under 2,000, presented no numerical threat to the AFL; whatever momentum was being gained by the socialist movement in the USA was going the way of Eugene Debs and the SPA – a movement to which De Leon was implacably hostile. In April 1904 De Leon had given an address on 'The Burning Question of Trades Unionism' in Newark, New Jersey. It was one of his finest speeches, and it marked a development in his thinking about the importance of trade unionism. The unions were to be seen as instruments of revolution, but, concluded De Leon with understandable pessimism, 'That day is not yet. The road thither may be long or short, but it is arduous. At any rate, we are not yet there.'[1] Little could De Leon have known as he made that statement that what he was saying would lay the intellectual foundation for a movement greater than any other with which he would be involved: the Industrial Workers of the World (IWW).

In 'The Burning Question of Trades Unionism' De Leon examined, by means of a fictitious dialogue, the case for and against trade union membership. The case 'for' consisted of the valid recognition that without combination the employers could do as they pleased with their workers. The case 'against' was based upon the claim that only negligible defence can be provided by pure and simple unions. The anti-unionist succeeds in crushing the false hopes of the pro-unionist, but the latter, reflecting what De Leon saw as the historically pertinent perspective, asserts that 'As sure as a man will raise his hand by mere instinct, to shield himself against a blow, so surely will workingmen, instinctively, periodically gather into unions. The union is the arm that labor instinctively throws up to screen its head.'[2] In short, the class struggle is not a voluntary but an inevitable, phenomenon in a society of conflicting class interests.

Given that unions are not 'smashable', De Leon faced up to a dilemma. The trade union is the main, instinctively grasped weapon of the working class, yet in its pure and simple form it is an impotent weapon, or, worse still, a potent instrument of self-enslavement. How can the role of unions be transformed? First, the union members must be made conscious of the nature of 'the weapon of assault' against which they throw up their arms to defend their heads; the labour lieutenant of capital has an interest 'to keep enlightenment from the masses', but the unions could not be so perverted 'if the rank and file of the union were enlightened'.[3] Secondly, the trade union movement cannot survive without the political party serving as a head of the lance, the function of which is to inject social consciousness into the workers in their instinctively created movement. The unions – the shaft in De Leon's metaphor – would be lost without the political head. But – and this is the new and crucial aspect of De Leon's theory – the political party cannot achieve victory without the revolutionised unions. This marks a fundamental break with the social-democratic theory of socialist transformation, which places the political party, bidding to win control of the state, as the principal vehicle for changing society. It was in 1904 that De Leon expressed his recognition of the limitation of such revolutionary theory:

> The majority of the voters are workingmen. But even if this majority were to sweep the political field on a classconscious, that is, *bona fide* labor or Socialist ticket, they would find the Capitalists able to throw the country into the chaos of a panic and to famine, unless they, the workingmen, were so well organized in the shops that they could laugh at all shut-down orders, and carry on production.[4]

To achieve this 'general lock-out of the Capitalist Class', as De Leon was later to call it, required a revolutionary industrial wing to the revolutionary political party:

> Thus we see that the head of the lance of the Socialist Movement is worthless without the shaft . . . we see that the one needs the other, that while the head – the political movement – is essential in its way, the shaft of the lance – the industrial movement – is requisite to give it steadiness. The labor movement that has not a well-pointed political lance-head can never rise above the babe condition in which the union is originally born; on the other hand, unhappy the political movement of labor that has not the shaft of the trades union organization to steady it. It will inevitably become a freak affair. The head of the lance may 'get there', but unless it drags in its wake the trades unions it will have 'got there' to no purpose.[5]

This amounted to far more than a shift in literary rhetoric: it was a new theory of revolution. Before 1904 De Leon saw the establishment of socialism as an act of political accomplishment. The SLP was the sword, the unions merely the shield. By the time De Leon had completed his revised thinking on this question (in 1907), the metaphors were reversed and the revolutionary unions became the sword, leaving the political party as a mere shield.

Why did De Leon adopt this new view? One explanation is that frustration, indeed desperation, arising from failure at the ballot-box, led him to look elsewhere for the potential ground of revolutionary activity. After nearly a decade and a half of electoral failure, De Leon was reaching the view that it would be easier to revolutionise the workers where vast numbers were organised already than in a political party which could attract only the more intellectually motivated. In the early 1900s syndicalist ideas were in the air, not only in the USA, but also in Europe. Syndicalism is a theory advocating revolutionary change by trade union action only. Political action, especially when defined as legal or parliamentary activity, was dismissed by the syndicalists. De Leon was far from being a syndicalist and, as we shall see, he was to put up a vigorous Marxist fight against their repudiation of political action. But he was attracted to their revolutionary zeal; their total rejection of pure and simple unionism; and their commitment to the all-important abolition of the wages system. These factors drew De Leon close to the new unions such as the Western Federation of Miners, led by Boyce and 'Big' Bill Haywood; the American Railway Union, led by Debs; and the United Brewery Workers, led by William Trautmann. Like the STLA, these were dual unions, despised by Gompers and the AFL bureaucracy. De Leon was an ardent reader of the United Brewery Workers' journal, the *Bauer Zeitung*, which was edited by Trautmann, a committed syndicalist. Between January and March 1905 the *Daily People* republished seven of Trautmann's articles putting the case for revolutionary unionism. De Leon was also influenced by Herbert Lagardelle's syndicalist tract, *Le Mouvement Socialiste*. So it was that, by the beginning of 1905, although the SLP was opposed in theory both to syndicalist and left-wing SPA members who were fighting for the revolutionary unionist position against the likes of Hillquit, in practice there was a thawing of the old antagonism. The *Daily People* was seen as the newspaper which supported militant trade unionism against AFL class-collaborationism, and for once De Leon resisted the temptation to turn his back on those who, though not with him, were going his way. The American Labor Union, formed in 1902, regarded De Leon as a major influence on the new industrial unionism, and it would be fair to credit him with laying the main theoretical foundation for what was to become the IWW.

De Leon's most trusted comrade at this time – the man being primed to take over the *People*'s editorship – was Frank Bohn, the SLP's national organiser. Bohn toured the country in the years 1904–5, speaking and organising even more than De Leon. In January 1905 it was Bohn, not De Leon, who was invited to Chicago to discuss and sign the Industrial Union Manifesto, a document which was seen by the SLP, according to Rudolph Katz, as not only arousing 'the working class spirit of class consciousness among men who had formerly not been reached by the advocates of revolutionary unionism' but also 'as a realization and acceptance of all that Daniel De Leon had taught and insisted upon'.[6] The Manifesto was a battle-cry against the old trade unionism, stating that 'Craft divisions foster political ignorance among the workers, thus dividing that class at the ballot box as well as in shop, mine and factory.'[7] Those agreeing with the Manifesto's principles were invited to a Convention in Chicago on 27 June 1905.

De Leon's enthusiasm for the Chicago Convention which was to form the IWW cannot be overstated. The evidence of his correspondence shows that he prepared for it in readiness for the most exciting of political developments. The minutes of the convention, which De Leon had stenographically recorded and the SLP published verbatim, make clear that De Leon's role was one of major influence in moulding the form of the new movement. Kuhn was doubtlessly right when he wrote how

> De Leon participated [in the founding of the IWW] with all the ardor of his soul, believing that, at last, the hour had struck that would see the working class, in larger numbers than ever before, take the first step towards the formation of a formidable organization on the economic field, based upon the unqualified recognition of the class struggle, and all that that implies.[8]

De Leon's presence at the Convention, together with twelve other STLA delegates, was characterised by an intense concern not to give sectarian offence. He realised that SLPers were in a minority. The Western Federation of Miners' five delegates represented 27,000 workers; the American Labor Union affiliated 16,780 workers; the United Metal Workers, 3,000; the United Brotherhood of Railway Employees, 2,087; the STLA, merely 1,450. De Leon was aware that he was personally disliked: SPA delegates to the Convention felt ill at ease entering into comradeship with their greatest of enemies. At the SLP's Tenth Convention, De Leon had referred scathingly to 'a crook like Debs'.[9] In Chicago Debs was the star attender and De Leon was eager not to snub him. For example, on one day of the Convention De Leon, overwhelmed by the heat of the city, retired to his hotel room; but so concerned was he that Debs might arrive in his absence and interpret his non-presence as a calculated insult, that he maintained constant telephone contact with the Convention hall so that he could rush in if Debs arrived. James Connolly, who had his own particular reasons for mistrusting De Leon, claimed that De Leon saw 'the IWW only as a body which ought to act as an auxiliary to bring recruits to the SLP . . .'.[10] He only wrote what others suspected.

But a less cynical, more generous, interpretation of De Leon's involvement in the establishment of the IWW is that he saw it as a movement bigger and more significant than the SLP. Of course, he wanted to inject into it SLP and STLA principles, but, in line with his thinking in 'The Burning Question of Trades Unionism' – which, as we have seen, pre-ceeded any plan for an IWW – De Leon was now of the view that the function of a political party was of lesser revolutionary value than that of a conscious, revolutionary, mass industrial union movement. Looked at this way, De Leon's zest for rank and file unity was less a calculated tactic than a recognition that on the industrial field the force of unity was a greater prize than precision of political analysis.

At the Convention Debs of the SPA and De Leon of the SLP extended friendly sentiments to one another. In his utter condemnation of the pure and simple AFL and its leader, Gompers, Debs was far closer to the SLP than to his fellow leaders in the SPA. (The latter would deal with Debs on that count at a later date.) Gompers had attacked Debs, leading De Leon to respond that that 'makes us fraternal already'.[11] Of the STLA, Debs remarked that 'I have not in the past agreed with their tactics', although 'their theory is right' and 'their princi-ples are sound'. He also made clear, in the face of those who regarded anybody emanating from the SLP as highly suspect, that he accepted 'the honesty of their membership'. Unlike others in the SPA, 'Upon my lips there has never been a sneer for the Socialist Trade and Labour Alliance on account of the smallness of its numbers.' He applauded their courage, 'for though few in numbers, they stay by their colors'. So, what was Debs's criticism of the STLA, and, by implication, De Leon? It was a rejection of their apparent sectarianism: 'that they are too prone to look upon a man as a fakir [faker] who happens to disagree with them'. So opposed to the 'labor fakers' were the De Leonists; so eager to find and expose them, that they see 'the fakir where the fakir is not'. Debs proceeded to the essence of his disagreement with De Leonism: 'I would have you understand that I am opposed to the fakir, and I am also opposed to the fanatic . . . And fanaticism is as fatal to the development of the working class movement as is fakirism.'. The meaning of all this was not obscure. De Leon had called Debs a 'fakir'. Of De Leon, Debs acknowledged that 'We have not been the best of friends in the past . . .', but 'A man is not worthy . . . to enlist in the services of the working class unless he has the moral stamina . . . to break asunder all personal relations to serve that class as he understands his duty to that class . . . I have not the slightest feeling against those who in the past have seen fit to call me a fakir.'[12] In short, the urgency of the movement must overcome past grievances; but De Leon and his men must desist from the 'fanatical' adherence to principles which had made enemies of those who should have been fighting together. Such words were like music to De Leon's ears. He, too, needed to put past feuding behind him in order to reach the necessary compromise which could turn the IWW into the revolutionary 'shaft' without which the revolutionary political party would 'inevitably become a freak affair'.

When De Leon rose to address the Convention, it was the speech of one who had been re-admitted to the club of working-class leaders, filled with sentiments of unity and measured humility:

> When I came to Chicago . . . I came absolutely without any private grudge to satisfy . . . during this process of pounding one another we have both learned; both sides have learned, and I hope and believe that this Convention will bring together those who will plant themselves squarely upon the class struggle . . . I recognise the courtesy of those who have called upon me [to speak] after Brother Debs' speech, and I wish here solemnly to state that whoever stands frankly and openly with his face turned

against the Capitalist Class . . . that man will find nothing but fraternal greeting from me as an individual and from the organization which I represent here.[13]

Was this the old, sectarian De Leon that delegates were hearing? Or were the whispers from his enemies right in urging listeners to dismiss the Convention sentiments and recognise De Leon's aim in using the IWW to build the SLP? The truth is more complex. The IWW signalled a change in the militant section of the trade union movement towards recognition of the class struggle and its revolutionary implications. Before such a change De Leon was isolated; now he had good reason to believe that his ideas were close to those of many American workers and, uninspired by any desire to dominate them, he threw himself into their struggle.

After the Convention De Leon embarked upon a Mid-Western speaking tour. In Minneapolis, Minnesota on 10 July, two days after the Convention closed, he delivered a speech entitled 'The Preamble of the IWW'. He was just the person to speak on the subject, for he had been a member of the Convention's Platform Committee and had written the famous Preamble. Perhaps intoxicated by the excitement of the historical moment, De Leon gave one of his most celebrated speeches ever. 'Big' Bill Haywood wrote to him from Denver, Colorado on 18 November enthusing that:

> I have read and re-read your Minneapolis address on the Preamble of the Industrial Workers of the World. Your exposition of the aims and objects of the IWW is clear and convincing. I wish that a copy of it could be placed in the hands of every man and woman of the working class in this country.[14]

The address in question, later published with the title, 'Socialist Reconstruction of Society' was in part a replication of De Leon's main speech at the Convention. This demonstrates

87

that he used well-structured notes when speaking, which enabled him to repeat fine points of detail and analogy in order, in a manner in which a spontaneous orator could not have done.

De Leon sought to explain the validity of three central clauses in the IWW's Preamble. The first two rested upon elementary Marxian economics, which De Leon illustrated with his customary simplicity. The first clause asserted that poverty and misery for the many, alongside affluence and privilege for the few, would be inevitable while 'the few, who make up the employing class, have all the good things in life'. Using government figures, De Leon illustrated how the prosperity of the capitalists is reflected in the poverty of the wage slaves: with poverty increasing not only quantitatively, but also qualitatively. 'The condition of the working class has gone from bad to worse.'[15]

The second clause, that 'The working class and the employing class have nothing in common', was discussed by De Leon with a view to showing the one-sidedness of the power relationship involved in the employment contract. The relationship between the employer and the employee is that 'between the vampire and the victim, whose blood it drains – and such relations surely establish nothing in common'. Those who 'prate about the "mutuality", the "brotherhood", the "identity" of interests of the capitalist, or employing class, and the working class . . . want of you that you believe it possible to divide an apple between two men in such a way that each shall have the bigger chunk'.[16] The worker is contracted to the capitalist, not freely, but only by 'the whip of hunger,'[17]

It was the third clause that De Leon chose to examine which was of the greatest significance in defining the political character of the IWW:

Between these two classes a struggle must go on until all the toilers come together on the political, as well as on the industrial field, and take and hold that which they produce by their labour through an economic organisation of the working class, without affiliation with any political party.

At the IWW Convention this formulation was the subject of much debate. Algie Simons of the SPA considered it unacceptably contradictory for the Preamble to declare in favour of working-class unity on the political field 'without affiliation with any political party'. How could there be political unity without a political party? The answer to this was that, there being two political parties in the USA claiming to be the true socialists, it would be better explicitly to rule out affiliation to one or the other. The hope was that the IWW might, in time, create its own political party. Those like Simons objected to the non-affiliation clause because they suspected that, with SPA members such as Debs and Haywood leading the IWW, the clause had been included by De Leon to prevent the new union from allying itself with the SPA as, for instance, the Western Federation of Miners had done. It would have been supremely ironic, however, for SPA members, whose principal criticism of De Leon was his mistaken tactic of effectively tying the STLA to the SLP in 1896, now to attack him for taking the opposite position. On the other hand, the 'political clause', as it became known, was criticised by anarchists and syndicalists who saw no need for a political struggle. In 1905 they remained in the minority.

It was between 1905 and 1908, during his membership of and influence upon the IWW, that De Leon elaborated his theory of revolution – or, to put it plainly, his ideas about how to get from capitalism to socialism. It is in this area of thought that De Leon is usually regarded as having made his most original contribution to socialist ideas. This is known as De Leon's

Theory of Socialist Industrial Unionism.

The theory rests upon the fundamental premise that the working class runs society from top to bottom. In De Leon's words:

> All the plants of production, aye, even the vast wealth for consumption, is today in the keeping of the working class. It is workingmen who are in charge of the factories, the railroads, the mines, in short all the land and machinery of production, and it is they also who sit as watchdogs before the pantries, the cellars and the safe-deposit vaults of the capitalist class; aye, it is they who carry the gun in the armies.[19]

De Leon's theory of revolution begins with the workers in a position of enormous power. Numerically, they constitute a majority. They produce all goods and services. They serve as managers, police and armed soldiers. But capitalism deprives those who contribute all of this to society from ownership and control of the means and instruments of wealth production and distribution. It is the capitalist minority which owns and controls, growing rich by exploiting the workers. The wage slaves' instinctive defence is trade unionism,.

Defenders of capitalism want to keep politics out of the union, but, argued De Leon, economic organisation is inescapably political: '. . . Socialist economics *is* politics. *By the same token capitalist economics is politics.*'[19] In the pure and simple craft unions capitalist economics is 'tolerated', 'safeguarded' and 'fought for'.[20] De Leon dismissed as 'an abstract question'[21] the issue of whether economic organisation gives rise to political awareness or political consciousness spurs industrial militancy. Before 1904 he held the conventional social-democratic view that politics is the sword and trade unionism the shield. By the time of his Minneapolis address in 1905, he had changed and asserted that 'the political movement is . . . the reflex of economic organization'.[22] 'It is not a political organization . . . that

90

can "take and hold" the land and the capital and the fullness thereof. That . . . is the function reserved for the economic organization of the working class.'[23] The role of the political party is to destroy capitalist power by means of building working-class consciousness and voting capitalist leaders out of power via the legal ballot. Once this 'destructive' mission is accomplished, the political wing of the socialist movement dissolves itself and the economic wing, being based at the point of production, takes and holds the social resources and attends to the 'constructive' work of reorganising society.

De Leon argued that his revolutionary theory was based on a position stated by Marx in an alleged interview given to Haman of the German metal workers' union in 1869. In this 'interview' Haman quoted Marx as stating that 'If the trades unions really want to accomplish their task, they must never associate themselves with any political unions or become dependent upon them in any way.' Instead, the trade unions must set the pace for the building of a worker's party: 'Only the economic organization is capable of setting on foot a true political party of Labor, and, thus raise a bulwark against the power of Capital.'[24] It is possible that Haman forged the interview with Marx or doctored his answers; De Leon was asked by his critics to show where Marx had ever written in favour of the primacy of the economic over the political movement, but was unable to do so, returning each time to Marx's position as reported by Haman. Ironically, the same critics who disowned the Haman reference when De Leon used it to defend his socialist industrial union position had previously used the quotation as a Marxist stick with which to beat De Leon when he had advocated the dependence of the STLA upon the SLP.

This revolutionary scenario contrasts with three others which De Leon opposed. First, anarchism: although that term meant and still means many things, in terms of the revolutionary overthrow of capitalism, De Leon took it to mean the process whereby a minority, using physical force, attempts to emancipate the workers by means of violent action to remove the current occupants of the state. In his lecture, *Socialism versus Anarchism*, given after the assassination of President McKinley by the anarchist, Leon Czolgosz, in 1901, De Leon argued that such tactics for revolution reflected the capitalist view of history with its authoritarian assumption 'that conditions can be changed by the mere decapitation of governments', as if 'government is something outside, separate and apart from the people'.[25] Against this, De Leon argued that 'You must educate the masses first . . . You must take the individual and revolutionize him. The revolutionising of the individual develops the necessary head which society requires to progress.'[26] In short, revolution must come from below, not from above, on behalf of those who are to be liberated.

Secondly, De Leon was opposed to syndicalism, a theory which he associated with French social conditions. 'American would-be imitators of "syndicalism"', he argued, should realise that such a theory of revolution would be as out of place in the USA as 'Polar bears under the tropics'.[27] The syndicalists argued that workers organised into 'One Big Union' could overthrow capitalism without the need for a political party or the use of the ballot.

Thirdly, De Leon rejected the notion of a solely political transformation of society, via the conventional parliamentary process. He derided

that curious apparition – the visionary politician, the man who imagines that by going to the ballot box, and taking a piece of paper, and looking about to see if anybody is watching, and throwing it in and then rubbing his hands and jollying himself with the expectation that through the process, through some mystic alchemy, the ballot will terminate capitalism, and the Socialist Commonwealth will arise like a fairy out of the ballot box.[28]

This was an undisguised reference to the outlook of those in the SPA who sought to legislate socialism into existence via Congress and municipal government.

Being neither a syndicalist who rejected political action nor a social-democrat who interpreted 'politics' in the traditional European socialist sense, De Leon was obliged to explain why it was necessary for workers to be active upon the political field. He answered this question at length during the debate on the political clause at the 1905 inaugural Convention of the IWW, and it is worth quoting his comments before examining the criticisms which were to be put by IWW anarchists and syndicalists in 1907–8, when the political clause came under attack:

The aspiration to unite the workers upon the political field is an aspiration in line and in step with civilization. Civilized man, when he argues with an adversary, does not start with clenching his fist and telling him, 'smell this bunch of bones'. He does not start by telling him, 'feel my biceps'. He begins by arguing; physical force by arms is the last resort. That is the method of the civilized man, and the method of civilized man is the method of civilized organization. The barbarian begins with physical force; the civilized man ends with that, when physical force is necessary. [Applause] Civilized man will always here in America give a chance to peace; he will, accordingly, proceed along the lines that make peace possible. But civilized man, unless he is a visionary, will know that unless there is Might behind your Right, your Right is something to laugh at. And the thing to do, consequently, is to gather behind the ballot, behind that united political movement, the Might which is alone able, when necessary, to 'take and hold'. Without the working people are united on the political field; without the delusion has been removed from their minds that any of the issues of the capitalist class can do for them permanently, or even temporarily; without the working people have been removed altogether from the mental thraldom of the capitalist class, from its insidious influence, there is no possibility of your having those conditions under which they can really organize themselves economically in such a way as to 'take and hold'. And after those mental conditions are generally established, there needs something more than the statement to 'take and hold'; something more than a political declaration, something more than the capitalist political inspectors to allow this or that candidate to filter through. You then need the industrial organization of the working class, so that if the capitalist should be foolish enough in America to defeat, to thwart the will of the workers expressed by the ballot – I do not say 'the will of the workers, as returned by the capitalist election inspectors', but the will of the people as expressed at the ballot box – then there will be a condition of things by which the working class can absolutely cease production, and thereby starve out the capitalist class, and render their present economic means and all their preparations for war absolutely useless. [Applause][29]

So, De Leon's theory of revolution postulated three stages: civilised debate, culminating in socialists winning the battle of ideas; victory at the ballot-box; and socialist industrial unions supplying the economic might to enforce electoral victory and workers' power. The advantage of this proposition was that it envisaged a legal, democratic and relatively peaceful social transformation.

De Leon was not of the view that his revolutionary theory could be applied everywhere: 'In no country, outside of the United States, is this theory applicable . . . no other country is ripe for the execution of Marxian revolutionary tactics',[30] he asserted in his Minneapolis address. (He conceded that 'Great Britain and the rest of the English-speaking world' could possibly be ripe for such tactics.) The reason for this American exceptionalism related to his theory of European semi-feudalism which, as we have seen, made him tolerant towards European reformism. In De Leon's view, the European ruling class, because of its feudal traditions, was a fighting class: 'Take as a type the semicrazy, semicrippled Emperor of Germany. He will fight whatever the odds. In Europe a peaceful solution of the social question is out of all question.' The American capitalists grew rich and powerful not with a spirit of nobility, manliness and valour, but

> by putting sand into your sugar, by watering their stocks, by putting shoddy into your clothes, by pouring water into your molasses, by breaches of trust, by fraudulent failures and fraudulent fires, in short by swindle . . . Let the political temperature rise to the point of danger, then . . . your capitalist will quake in his stolen boots; he will not dare to fight; he will flee.'[31]

It is on the basis of this historical expectation that De Leon contended that in the USA, more than anywhere else on earth, the socialist revolution could occur peacefully. He was not suggesting that voting was sufficient or that violent defence of the majority will must be ruled out, but that, supported by revolutionary, socialist industrial unions, the capitalist minority could be locked out and rendered powerless without a shot being fired. The creation of the IWW gave substance to this hope of peaceful revolution.

So, why did De Leon's theory of revolution come under attack? Why was it that in November 1906 the *People* opened its column to a public debate on revolutionary strategy which was to last until February 1907? (The latter correspondence was published as a pamphlet with the title *As To Politics*.) The first reason was that there were anarcho-syndicalists in the IWW who had a principled theoretical objection to the case for political action. They bombarded De Leon with such questions as 'Are the workers a majority?'; 'Even if they are, could not the capitalist constitutionalists disqualify certain workers from

95

voting or, more importantly, count out revolutionary votes?' The anarchist, Arturo Giovannitti, quoting Sorel, suggested that to use in any way the capitalist state to achieve socialist victory is a form of collaboration with the old regime. In Giovannitti's view, 'It is then by main force and through violence only that we can transform society, but collective, organized violence . . .'.[32] This view had been put at the inaugural Convention of the IWW, when Delegate Bartlett argued against the 'political clause' and declared that 'You can vote better probably with machine guns and hand grenades in the course of time.'[33]

In one sense, these theoretical disputations about strategy were relatively insignificant. They were potentially splitting conflicts about what exactly would happen once the workers were ready for socialism, and had little to do with immediate tactics. As James Connolly said when asked whether he favoured the IWW dropping the call for political action in its Preamble, 'It will be impossible to prevent the workers taking it.'[34]

De Leon's theory of 'peaceful revolution' was put under strain more by material factors than by theoretical challenges. The fact was that the IWW was taking a vicious beating from the American capitalists wherever it pursued its struggle against them. The fine story of the Wobblies and their courageous battle against the oppressive might of exploiting capital is not within the scope of this book but it will suffice to state that it was an intensely bloody battle, with violence and trickery nearly always initiated by the bosses. They were hard times to preach peaceful revolution. John Sandgren of San Francisco, one of De Leon's most competent antagonists in the debate *As To Politics*, asked:

> But why speak of peace or war! The capitalist class has already chosen war. Our blood has run in torrents, as in the Paris

Commune, or bespattered the road to Hazelton and Cripple Creek; the rope has strangled some of our early champions and is in preparation for others. To speak of a possibility of peaceable settlement between us and the master class is the same as the mutual agreement between the man flat on his back and the man who holds the dagger to his throat.[35]

Sandgren had grasped the mood of the moment. V. H. Kopald, in his contribution, agreed that 'we live now in a state of war, a war of classes. It was always a maxim of war: Do what the enemy does not want you to do'.[36] The enemy favours a political, electoral struggle, so the IWW must abandon it. De Leon responded that war as such did not yet exist, for otherwise the IWW could not have organised an open Convention and the *People*'s correspondence could not be conducted openly. This had a hollow ring to it at a time when Haywood and Moyer of the Western Federation of Miners were locked in prison cells, framed on a murder charge upon the bribed evidence of one Harry Orchard, a known criminal liar. Debs was warning that if these IWW leaders were murdered by the state, armed workers would respond: it would not be like twenty years earlier when the state killed the Haymarket Martyrs and labour was too disorganised to rise in their defence. So, even if De Leon was advocating the right theory of revolution, he was doing so at the wrong time.

It would be useful to summarise De Leon's responses to his *As To Politics* opponents, so as to clarify exactly what he was arguing as opposed to what he seemed to be saying. Throughout the debate, De Leon persisted in asking a question, the answer to which is crucial to any revolutionary strategy: how do you win over workers to the socialist cause? For De Leon, the answer was clear: persuasion, education, 'revolutionising the individual' on a mass scale. This requires principled and well-organised propaganda. That is the first role of the

97

political party: to act as propagandist for socialist ideas. Without such political agitation, what is the alternative? An insufficiently conscious working class, which, lacking socialist education, would turn to physical force as a means of fighting capitalism. Without the organised force of revolutionary ideas as its weapon, the working class would descend to the brute violence of the capitalist. The importance which De Leon attached to so-called civilised methods could give rise to the charge that he was possessed by bourgeois moral scruples. After all, did not the early utopian socialists like Fourier expose the utter sham and worthlessness of civilisation? Giovannitti accused De Leon of using 'civilised' as a euphemism for 'legal'. This allegation was disposed of: '*The People* is not troubled with the thought of "legality."*The People* planted itself upon the principle of "civilization".' How does this principle manifest itself? De Leon explained:

> Giovannitti and the Editor of *The People* are civilized men. Being civilized men they are discussing the subject politely. Were the two a couple of barbarians they would have begun by breaking each other's heads . . . Political action is the civilized, because it is the peaceful method of social debate and of ascertaining numbers. He who rejects that method places himself upon the barbarian plane, a plane where the capitalist would be too glad to see him, seeing that he would thereby give the capitalist class a welcome pretext to drop all regard for decency and resort to the terrorism that would suit it.[37]

For De Leon, then, peace was preferable to violence. It was not a moral preference, but a practical one. Violence is the revolutionary method of the capitalist class. Socialism, being a peaceful, co-operative end, must be established by means compatible with such an end. De Leon warned his anarchist opponents not to separate means and ends: for example, Karl Marx had asserted that 'force is the midwife of every old society pregnant with a new one'; according to Giovannitti, De Leon jested, 'all that is needed for the birth of a child is the midwife; the function of the father and the mother count for nothing'.[38]

Just as 'civilised' was read by some as meaning 'legal', 'political action' was read as meaning mere electorialism. In his Minneapolis address, De Leon quoted William Liebknecht's maxim, 'to parliamentarize is to compromise, to logroll, to sell out',[39] Again, in *As To Politics*, he wrote that 'The emancipation of the proletariat, that is, the Socialist Republic, can not be the result of legislative enactment. No bunch of office-holders will emancipate the proletariat.'[40] As for the ballot, its value 'as a constructive force is zero'.[41] To portray De Leon as an advocate of conventional 'politics' would be a serious misreading of his advocacy of 'political action'. For De Leon, the importance of political agitation lay in its function of facilitating thoughtful, peaceful movement. Thus motivated, the workers could enter the political field, but not in order to engage in primaries or Conventions 'or any other established method for the nomination of candidates for office in the "political", that is, the "class rule" government'.[42] Socialist political agitation would involve voting, but for principles, not candidates:

> Accordingly, the Socialist Labor Party says not to the working-men: Vote the Socialist Labor Party ticket. It explains to them why they should vote that ticket, and it adds, If you do not yet understand why, then, for heaven's sake, cast not your votes with us.[43]

The above was stated in 1901, before De Leon had evolved his Socialist Industrial Union theory of revolution, but it was fully applicable to his view of politics during the IWW years. The crucial factor is the appeal to mass consciousness, which was the key, in De Leon's view, to real change. On the other hand, organisation for an insurrectionary overthrow of capitalism – which is what 'physical force' amounted to in practice – would inevitably 'degenerate into "conspiracy"; conspiracy can be conducted in circumscribed localities only, such localities exclude the masses – and the wheels of time are turned back'.[44] So, political agitation is a propagandistic, educational exercise in recruiting workers to socialist ideas, using elections and all other opportunities for public discussion about society to do so.

The aim of socialist political agitation is to win a working-class majority, and, hence, an overall majority in the USA according to De Leon's reckoning, to commit themselves in favour of socialism. De Leon envisaged three possible revolutionary scenarios. First, the SLP wins at the hustings on the basis of demanding the unconditional surrender of the capitalist class. The election officers count the votes fairly and acknowledge the socialist victory, in which case 'the SLP would forthwith dissolve; the political state would be *ipso facto* abolished' and power would pass to the workers themselves in their industrial unions. Such a peacefully democratic change of power, De Leon considered 'highly improbable'.[45] This pessimism was a change from his earlier position – or perhaps it was a concession to the anarcho-syndicalists. In 1892 De Leon had asserted that:

> Thanks to universal suffrage it [the working class] can take them [the state institutions] now, peacefully, in one day, by a mere declaration of its will at the ballot box.
>
> Nor can its will be frustrated. No despot was ever able to successfully challenge the majority of a nation when that majority, conscious of its right, aware of its strength, was determined to assert itself.[46]

Now, De Leon put the view that consciousness of right must have the backing of the union's might.

The second scenario is that there is a socialist election victory, but the socialist majority is 'counted out': the capitalists fix the election. In this case, political agitation ceases and the socialist movement turns to its economic organisation, the IWW. By acting in a democratic and peaceful way before then, the SLP had been allowed to exist and recruit revolutionary-minded members for the IWW, but once the capitalist play foul with the ballot, the socialists would have to go 'to the last resort, and physically mop the earth with the barbarian Capitalist Class'.[47] De Leon was clearly no pacifist.

The third, and most likely, revolutionary scenario, in De Leon's view, was that 'the political expression of the IWW will not be afforded the time for triumph at the polls'. Before the time that a socialist electoral victory could be achieved, the IWW would be driven to employ force against the ruling class. 'A strike will break out; capitalist brutality will cause the strike to spread; physical, besides moral support, will pour in from other and not immediately concerned branches of the working class.'[48] In short, the capitalists could provoke open warfare, as they had done against the striking miners in 1902 and in the 1904 Pullman Strike. De Leon was not confident about how such a situation would develop. (This is unusual; revolutionaries are usually confident, for the sake of morale, even when such an attitude is quite groundless.) If, at such a time, the IWW was sufficiently organised and peopled by conscious socialists, then victory could be won; if not, the workers would be defeated. This neatly returns to De Leon's original point: unless there was political agitation to recruit class-conscious members, the IWW could not act as a revolutionary force.

One final point should be made regarding De Leon's theory of revolution: the political party which he argued would play a crucial, if secondary, role in the revolutionary process need not be the SLP. In 1906–7, when De Leon was participating in the *As To Politics* debate, the SLP was the only party to endorse the IWW fully. The SPA was split on the matter: its Right supported Gompers's AFL; its Left was behind the IWW; and a broad Centre admired the IWW but feared its vote-losing revolutionary ideas, not to mention its association with De Leon. The latter regarded three political developments as possible: the SPA could be won over by its left wing and merge with the SLP, then to be adopted by the IWW; the SPA Leftists could leave, join the SLP and the latter could be adopted by the IWW 'as its political reflex'; or, the IWW could form its own, new, political party. If a new IWW Party was formed 'the SLP will "break up camp" with a shout of joy if a body merging into its own ideal can be said to "break up camp"'.[49]

All of this depended on the direction that the IWW would take. After Haywood's arrest and imprisonment in 1906, the Western Federation of Miners moved to the right, seeing excessive danger in the revolutionary rhetoric of the IWW. The WFM and other, less-militant, forces supported Charles O. Sherman, who had been elected President of the IWW in 1905, and who sought to exclude political literature from circulating in the union. De Leon, in alliance with Trautmann of the Brewers, and Vincent St John, the leading leftist in the WFM in Haywood's absence, used their voting strength at the 1906 IWW Convention to oust Sherman from the Presidency and to abolish the office altogether. In a manner reminiscent of the Kangaroos in 1899, Sherman and a few followers attempted to take over the IWW offices in Chicago and hijack the union. Sherman declared that 'The Convention was controlled by the SLP under the leadership of Daniel De Leon'.[50] This was an exaggeration, used by Sherman to discredit the IWW in the eyes of the right wing of the WFM and the SPA. Vincent St John's comment on the Shermanites was that 'they are, because of lack of argument with which to sustain a wrong position, hoping to cause the prejudice which exists against De Leon and the Socialist Labor Party to blind many to the true state of affairs . . .', namely, the Shermanites' attempt to diminish the militancy of the IWW.[51] Debs also defended De Leon's reputation, pointing out that 'opposition to the IWW, inspired by hatred for Daniel De Leon . . . is puerile to say the least . . . Most of the opposition to the IWW is centered upon the head of Daniel De Leon and has a purely personal animus.'[52]

In allying himself with anarcho-syndicalists like Trautmann and St John, De Leon was playing a dangerous game; in fact, he was setting himself up for his subsequent defeat by the syndicalist majority. At the 1906 IWW Convention, De Leon accepted a revision of the wording of the Preamble limiting the role of political action: 'Therefore, without endorsing any political party or desiring the endorsement of any political party, we unite under the following constitution . . ' read the new clause.

By 1907 the IWW was on the decline. The right-wing controlled WFM, in Haywood's absence, disaffiliated and overall membership was approximately 6,000 – hardly the 'might' depicted by De Leon's theory of revolutionary unionism. Paul Brissenden, the first historian of the Wobblies, suggests that De Leon 'managed' the 1907 IWW Convention.[53] It was at this Convention, however, that De Leon had to fight harder than ever to retain the political clause. 'It is begging the question to say that we want political action', he stated, trying to appease the syndicalists, 'we want our political reflex on the day so that we are strong enough, but we are not quite strong enough for political action now, we need a political shield'.[54] The motion to delete the political clause was lost, with only fifteen votes cast in favour and 113 against. In the same year, at the Stuttgart

103

Congress of the Second International, De Leon moved a motion of explicit support for socialist industrial unionism. It was seconded by Fred Heslewood, who sat as delegate for the IWW. A majority of the French votes were cast in support of the motion, as were those American votes not in the possession of the SPA, but it did not carry the day at the International.

Back in the USA the syndicalists were preparing their forces to remove the political clause at the IWW's Fourth Convention in 1908. In January De Leon personally attended the General Executive Board in New York City, of which he was not a member. His address was to the effect that the deletion of the clause would result in the seccesion of the Eastern-based Wobblies of the old STLA. His threat was to no avail. The principal IWW base was the West, and plans were made to bring in a large number of Western Wobblies to vote away the commitment to political action at the Chicago Convention. De Leon lost no time in attacking what he saw as an anarchist tendency; he called them 'slummists', 'the overall brigade' and 'the bummery' – on account of their song, 'Hallelujah, I'm a bum'. It would be hard to conceive of a wider cultural gulf than that between De Leon and the Western rank and file. He prided himself upon intellectual accomplishment; they were unashamedly anti-intellectualist and intolerant of ideologies. De Leon respected discipline; they saw themselves as uncontrollable, free spirits in the pioneer tradition. De Leon loathed violence; they lived with violence and meant it literally when they spoke of fighting the bosses. These rugged class warriors would not be impressed by De Leon's talk of civilised methods.

Before the Convention the syndicalist, Cole, published an article in the IWW's *Industrial Union Bulletin* daring De Leon to attend. Even threats of violence against SLPers were in the air. De Leon did attend, but his allies of times past, St John and

Trautmann, refused his delegate's credentials on a technicality. De Leon attended as a delegate for the New York City Office Workers' Local, when he should have been a member of the Print Workers' local. His right to sit was denied by forty votes to twenty-one. 'It is not me who is on trial before this Convention', stated De Leon, 'it is you who stand on trial. You who have to account for your actions at the bar of the international movement of the proletariat.'[55] The political clause was deleted.

On 1 November a number of Eastern IWW locals, mainly from New York and Paterson, New Jersey met to set up a new IWW, based upon the 1905 Preamble. The De Leonist IWW set up headquarters in Detroit, Michigan and became known as the Detroit IWW. Like the STLA before it, this new body was numerically weak and industrially of little significance. After 1908 the original IWW lost its intellectual substance: only three issues of the *Industrial Union Bulletin* appeared after the Convention and the movement, whilst fiercely militant in specific struggles, lost direction and therefore purpose.

With the split in the IWW came the end of De Leon's most promising hope of being influential upon a movement which could give substance to his revolutionary tactics. After 1908 De Leon was more committed than ever to the theory of Socialist Industrial Unionism, but theory it was to remain, and, as time passed, its distance from the actuality of the class struggle became more apparent. As we shall see, De Leon appealed unsuccessfully to Haywood, after the latter was released from prison, to revive the spirit of solidarity which had inaugurated the IWW. But in 1908, once again, De Leon was out in the cold.

6 The De Leon—Connolly conflict

James Connolly is widely known as a hero in the national struggle of Ireland. Many of those who celebrate him as a nationalist forget that Connolly was at one time a professed revolutionary socialist. Still less is it usually recalled that Connolly's socialist inclinations were not those of a labour reformist, but of a militant impossibilist. Connolly the Marxist was influenced above all by the ideas of Daniel De Leon.

Connolly, a native of Scotland, had joined William Morris's Socialist League in Dundee in 1888 or 1889. The League had split from the Hyndman-led Social Democratic Federation (SDF) in 1884; as I have shown elsewhere, Morris, Eleanor Marx, Aveling, Bax and the other League members left the SDF because of its position of possibilist compromise.[1] Like the post-1900 SLP in the USA, the League which Connolly joined did not advocate reforms and stood for 'pure and simple' socialism. With the demise of the League, Connolly joined and became Secretary of the Scottish Socialist Federation, which was affiliated to the SDF.

In the early 1900s Marxists in Britain began to be influenced by De Leon's writings. They were regarded as an exciting, uncompromising alternative to the ideas to be found in the SDF's own journal, *Justice*. In London, the impossibilist minority which was later to form the Socialist Party of Great Britain (SPGB) gathered in the North London Socialist Club in Finsbury and ordered from New York as much De Leonist literature as they could obtain. Jack Fitzgerald, who was later to play a key role in the formation of the SPGB, urged T.A. Jackson, who was a founder member of the same party, to subscribe to the *People*: 'This was, he thought, the best Socialist journal published in English. . .', Jackson recalls in his autobiography.[2] The larger group of impossibilists in the SDF, who were to remain more specifically De Leonist than their London counterparts, were in Scotland, mainly around Edinburgh. The most notable Scottish activists included George Yates, John Carstairs Matheson, William Walker and William Gee. The SDF leadership dubbed these impossibilists 'The Unholy Scotch Current'. Matters came to a head in the SDF over the same issue that had split the SLP in 1899: namely, reform versus revolution. The SDF leaders were courting the Independent Labour Party, which repudiated the class struggle; they sought support from the 'pure and simple' trade unions with their concern for nothing beyond the wages system; and in Paris in 1900 they supported the Kautsky resolution on Millerandism. In contrast with all of these strategic compromises and errors stood the fine example of the principled SLP, with De Leon serving as an inspiration to the revolutionary minority in the SDF. In 1902 the Edinburgh members launched their own journal, the *Socialist*, officially as the propaganda paper of the Scottish branches, but in reality as an outlet for De Leonist ideas.

The *Socialist* was printed on the press of James Connolly's Irish Socialist Republican Party (ISRP). By 1902 Connolly had fallen under the influence of De Leon's outlook. In February the *People* had serialised his *Erin's Hope*, and other writings by Connolly had met with De Leon's editorial favour. In turn, the *Socialist* serialised De Leon's 'What Means This Strike?' and republished many articles by De Leon. In August Connolly was formally invited by the SLP to visit the USA and speak for them. Connolly accepted eagerly. For De Leon, Connolly's presence would be a means of reaching out to the Irish immigrant workers whose political enthusiasm, like many immigrant groups before them, tended to be defused in romanticised nationalist movements. For Connolly, the trip was to be used to expose the capitalist nature of the Home rule Party before the Irish-American workers, who were the main source of its funding, and to obtain subscriptions for the ISRP's financially bankrupt journal, the *Workers' Republic*.

Connolly arrived in New York as a star guest of the SLP. The IWW had not yet been formed and De Leon was glad to meet a like-minded comrade. On 19 September the two men shared the platform at the Cooper Union in New York. The hall was packed full. 'I feel under a great disadvantage in addressing such a large and enthusiastic body of working men as are gathered here this evening', explained Connolly to the audience, 'though accustomed to addressing audiences of the working class in England, Scotland and my own country, I never stood before such a crowd before.'[3] The size and enthusiasm of the SLP impressed Connolly. He impressed them and they passed a resolution noting that his visit was to enlist 'the interest of Irish Americans in the Socialist movement and . . . destroy the influence of the Irish Home Rulers . . . who trade on the Irish vote in this country' and cordially welcoming him to the USA.[4] He was then sent on a nationwide speaking tour, taking both the indoor and the outdoor platforms across the USA to California.

In Salt Lake City, Utah, Connolly made some comments at a meeting which, according to his biographer, C.Desmond Greaves, 'may have started De Leon's dislike for Connolly'.[5] If it did, then why did De Leon publish the remarks in the *People*; and why did he welcome Connolly's return to the USA a year later? At the meeting Connolly was told by an SPA questioner the old story about how the tyrant, De Leon, had driven thousands out of the SLP. In response Connolly observed that 'De Leon struck me as a somewhat chirpy old gentleman with an inordinately developed bump of family affection.'[6] If anything, this was a compliment: Connolly had perceived De Leon as an amicable fellow and realised that the 1899 split had been about principles rather than personalities. Connolly also warned against 'the American national disease, swelled head'[7] which he thought that even the SLP suffered from. Perhaps he was referring to De Leon's theory that the socialist revolution would begin in the USA or De Leon's faith in the huge claims of the American Constitution. However this was taken, De leon shared the platform with Connolly in new York City on 2 January 1903 and joined in the wholehearted cheers for the Irish comrade.

If Connolly went to the USA under the influence of De Leon, he returned to Dublin a convert. 'I came back stronger than ever in my belief in our position, and in the general SLP analysis of its own enemies', he wrote to the Scottish impossibilist, Matheson, upon his return.[8] Back in Ireland Connolly was accused of 'bossism' by some members of the ISRP. Indeed, he must have fallen under De Leon's influence, even to the extent of attracting the same attacks. The anti-Connolly minority established their own Socialist Labor Party, which, according to Michael Rafferty, the ISRP's Secretary, writing to the American SLP, called itself the SLP in order 'to trade on the reputation gained by your party in America and the new party in Britain. . .'.[9] The new British party called the SLP was an impossibilist breakaway from the SDF, formed with the help of Connolly on 7 June 1903. In the June issue of the *Socialist*, which became the official organ of the SLP in Britain (the SLPGB), Connolly wrote an article entitled 'The SLP of America and the London SDF', in which he stated his reasons for adopting the De Leonist position:

> The SLP does everything the SDF has not the heart to do; it
> therefore shows its belief in its principles, and wins the respect of
> its enemies even whilst they hate it. On the other hand the SDF
> recoils from the logical application of the principles it professes to
> believe in.

Financial hardship led Connolly to return to the USA in
October 1903. He hoped that the SLP would offer him a paid
job, but none was offered. The capitalist economy was not
kind to Connolly during his six-year stay. After six months as
an active SLPer he found himself in conflict with De Leon, a
theoretical dispute which was to lead to bitter enmity.

On 9 april 1904 the *Weekly People* published a letter of criticism from Connolly entitled 'Wages, Marriage and the
Church'. Before examining the substance of the criticisms
raised, two points should be borne in mind. First, Connolly
began his letter by stating that 'I find myself in complete
accord with the SLP on all questions of policy and of discipline. . .'. At a time when De Leon and his party were overwhelmed by opposition, particularly in relation to the rejection
of palliatives and the tactic of dual unionism, Connolly was testi-
fying to his complete adherence to these central policies. His
complaint was that some 'party speakers and writers give
expression to conceptions of socialism with which I could not
agree'. The second point to note about this is that De Leon's
decision to publish such criticisms in the party journal was
incongruent with the image of a tyrannical, dogmatic sect
which permits no doubt amongst its members. De Leon disagreed with Connolly's criticisms, but he met them in public
so that readers could decide their merits for themselves.

Connolly's first criticism was of an economic nature. At a
meeting in Schenectady, New York, Connolly had crossed

swords with SLPers who denied the usefulness of gaining increased wages because these are offset by increased prices. Then Connolly attended another meeting 'in the West', at which an SLP speaker put the same argument against an SPA opponent. The SPA man quoted from Marx's *Value, Price and Profit* to prove that wage rises do not necessarily led to offsetting price rises, but 'our SLP man airily disposed of Marx by saying that Marx wrote in advance of and without anticipation of the present-day combination of capital. . .'. Connolly was of the view that 'the SLP speaker knew little of Marx except his name' and, whilst the claim that the wages struggle under capitalism is irrelevant to workers 'might sound very revolutionary', it is false and 'no part of our doctrine'. If it were valid, then the STLA would be reduced to 'little else than a mere ward heeling club for the SLP'.

The second criticism concerned the socialist attitude to monogamous marriage. When touring the USA in 1902, Connolly met in Indianapolis 'an esteemed comrade who almost lost his temper with me because I expressed my belief in monogamic marriage, and because I said I still hold the tendency of civilisation is towards its perfection and completion, instead of its destruction'. De Leon had serialised in the *People* Bebel's *Woman Under Socialism*, which he thought was a Marxist classic. He had translated the work, and the NYLN had purchased the copyright for it. In the Translator's Preface De Leon described the book as 'the best-aimed shot at the existing social system', for, in his view, the position of women under capitalism 'is the weakest link in the capitalist mail'.[10]

In his 9 April letter, Connolly expressed concern that the view of his Indianapolis comrade was 'held by a very large number of members'. They were 'wrong' and works such as Bebel's 'are an excrescence upon the movement'. Connolly was of the view that the abolition of capitalism would remove

111

only the economic handicaps faced by women, but 'men and women would still be unfaithful to their vows and questions of the intellectual equality of the sexes would still be as much in dispute as they are today. . .'. Furthermore, Connolly doubted if a single woman had been 'led to socialism' by reading Bebel's book, 'but you can find hundreds who were repelled from studying socialism by judicious extracts from its pages'. In short, socialists should avoid saying what might offend the moral sensibilities – sexist prejudices, we might call them – of those who were asked to become socialists.

Connolly's third – and surely not unrelated – point of criticism concerned the 'attitude of the party towards religion'. On 19 March the *People* had published an article by Emil Vandervelde, the Belgian social-democratic leader, entitled 'Socialism or the Catholic Church'. In it the writer referred to an increasing 'concentration of forces about the Catholic Church on the one side, the Social Democracy on the other. But none can deny that this concentration was inevitable, and that the future struggles will have to be fought out between these two armies.' Connolly, in his 9 April letter, complained that:

> It is scarcely possible to take up a copy of the *Weekly People* of late without realizing from its contents that it and the party are becoming distinctly anti-religious. If a clergyman anywhere attacks socialism the tendency is to hit back, not at his economic absurdities, but at his theology, with which we have nothing to do.

This policy of socialists not having any comment to make against religious beliefs and theology reflected that laid down by the German SPD at Erfurt in 1891: namely, that 'religion is a private matter'. Connolly endorsed this position: 'Theoretically every SLP man agrees that socialism is a political and economic question and has nothing to do with religion.' This was, indeed, the official position of the SLP, but one which

Connolly feared was being abandoned and replaced by atheistic materialism.

De Leon published his own reply to Connolly in the same issue. On marriage and religion he was on strong ground. Connolly's points on wages and prices were valid ones, even looked at from the perspective of De Leon's usual Marxist analysis. As has been demonstrated already, De Leon was not a Lassallean and should have accepted Connolly's criticisms regarding SLPers who were confused about the wage – price relationship. Instead, he quoted from Marx's *Value, Price and Profit* in a manner which was inaccurate, if not somewhat dishonest. He quoted Marx in support of the Connolly position 'that a general rise of wage *would* result in a fall in the general rate of profit, but *not* affect the average prices of commodities, or their values. . .', but then proceeded to quote Marx's question, 'how far, in this incessant struggle between capital and labour, the latter is likely to prove successful'. The answer which De Leon quoted from Marx, in support of the anti-Connolly position, was that 'despite all the ups and downs, and do what he may, the working man will on the average only receive the value of his labor, which resolves into the value of his laboring power which is determined by the value of the necessaries required for its maintenance and reproduction'. In fact, Marx had said rather more than that. Marx had preceded his answer with the words, 'I might answer by a generalisation. . .' and, after the quoted passage, went on to qualify this generalisation by pointing out 'some peculiar features which distinguish the value of the labouring power, or the value of labour, from the value of all other commodities'. This distinction was that labour power is a socially conscious commodity and its price, i.e. the wage obtained for selling labour power, is determined historically in accordance with traditions, habits and 'the respective powers of the combatants'.[11] It was in the latter role that De Leon defended the need for the STLA: it could prevent wages from being pushed down as much as they would be if there was no trade union organisation.

Having evaded the thrust of Connolly's economic criticism, De Leon felt on stronger ground dealing with religion. He denied that the SLP had devoted its columns to attacks upon theology. Like Connolly, De Leon endorsed the Erfurt position. 'With Daniel O'Connell, the SLP say – 'All the religion you like from Rome, but no politics.' (O'Connell had been an Irish Catholic capitalist politician.) Since the assassination of McKinley in 1901, the Catholic priests had been slandering the SLP, claiming that all socialists were murderers. De Leon had attacked the reasoning of such men, pointing out that it is their outlook which places power above the heads of human beings 'and by claiming that governmental power comes from above instead of from below, was, under given conditions, a natural breeder of assassins of rulers. . .'.[12] Without realising it, De Leon was admitting the impossibility of counteracting the Church's assault upon socialist ideas without attacking the theological basis of its thinking. But De Leon rejected Connolly's claim that the SLP was anti-religious, and even conceded that the article published by Vandervelde represented only the 'private opinions' of its author.

De Leon then proceeded to deal with Connolly's criticism of Bebel on marriage and the social role of women. He described as 'utopian' Connolly's view that only 'the economic side of the Woman question' will be solved by removing capitalism. Connolly was accused of 'projecting capitalist conditions into socialism'. As with religion, De Leon's own position on monogamy was not that far from Connolly's. We have already noted that he was vigorous in his support for female suffrage. In his Preface to *Woman Under Socialism* De Leon wrote of women under capitalism that, 'The shot that rips up the wrongs done to her touches a nerve that aches from end to end in the capitalist world. There is no woman, whatever her station, but in one way or other is a sufferer, a victim in modern society.'[13] In this view, De Leon was at one with Bebel, and Bebel in accord with Engels, whose study of gender roles had attributed female inferiority to social causation not natural factors. All were at one with Marx, who had stated that the degree to which any society is genuinely liberated can be judged by the role of women in it. But De Leon did not adhere dogmatically to Bebel's 'free love' outlook. He stated in the preface that:

> In a work of this nature, which . . . projects itself into hypotheses of the future, and even whose premises necessarily branch off into fields that are not essentially basic to Socialism, much that is said is, as the author himself announces in his introduction, purely the personal opinion of the writer.[14]

As to the future of monogamic marriage, De leon dissented from this 'personal opinion':

> For one, I hold that the monogamous family – bruised and wounded in the cruel rough-and-tumble of modern society, where. . . male creation is held down, physically, mentally and morally, to the brutalizing level of the brute, forced to grub and grub for bare existence . . . will have its wounds staunched, its bruises healed, and, ennobled by the slowly acquired moral forces of conjugal, paternal and filial affection, bloom under Socialism into a lever of mighty power for the moral and physical elevation of the race.[15]

What is clear from the substance, though not the tone, of De Leon's response to Connolly's criticisms is that the two men's ideas were not very far apart. On monogamous marriage they agreed. Connolly did not like Bebel's book and De

115

Leon did, but the the latter accepted that much in it was 'not essentially basic to Socialism' and only hypothetical.On religion, again, the two men both held tight to the Erfurt position, and opposed in principle the use of socialist literature to attack theology. Both men agreed that wage rises do not automatically cause price rises; De Leon quoted Marx to that effect, although he followed this up with some rather feeble economic reasoning, mainly intended, one suspects, to get his SLP comrades off of the theoretical hook which they had hung themselves upon. Connolly knew very well that De Leon did not hold the wages theory which he was attacking, and, to De Leon's intense discomfort, he subsequently quoted back at him his earlier published statement that:

> The theory that increased wages means increased prices, and that therefore an increase of wages through unionism is a barren victory, inasmuch as the men would have to pay for what they buy as much more than they get, is one frequently advanced by half-baked Marxists. The theory was never wholly correct; it is now substantially false.[16]

Given the actual similarity in their ideas, it is hard not to conclude that the De Leon–Connolly conflict was motivated more by mutual suspicion than real opposition. Connolly, perhaps, feared that De Leon had some sympathy for the 'iron law of wages'. We have shown, however, that De Leon was an opponent of the economic theory of Lassalle. Connolly also held the view that the socialist movement had in the past been 'hampered' by 'faddists and cranks' who sought to use it as 'a means of ventilating their theories on such questions as sex, religion, vaccination, vegetarianism, etc.'. For Connolly, such ideas 'ought to have no place in our programme or in our party'.[17] For his part, De Leon may well have suspected Connolly of being too eager to appeal to Catholic workers on their own anti-materialist terms, and of holding sexist views incompatible with the outlook of a social revolutionary. Such suspicions, easily bred within the confines of a minute party constantly conscious of the fragility of its tightly held principles, are more likely to account for the conflict than Katz's assertion that Connolly fell out with De Leon because he was a job-hunter and the SLP would not offer him employment; or Desmond Greaves's suggestion that De Leon was angered by the fact that Connolly raised a fundamental challenge to the tactics of the SLP.[18] This is hardly plausible, considering that Connolly began by declaring no less than 'complete accord with the SLP on all questions of policy and of discipline. . .'.

The 9 April clash gave rise to a vigorous correspondence in the *People*. Most contributors supported the De Leon reply. The letters on the wages question comprised amplifications of the De Leon position.[19] The Bebel book was defended: Patrick Twomey failed to see how 'after reading that book the majority of members of the SLP should favour plural marriages, or how enemies to socialism could be made by such reading'.[20] Carl Schluter opposed monogamus marriage on the grounds that 'love cannot be compelled and must be free'.[21]

On religion, Connolly's comments unleashed a materialist backlash. Twomey contended that: 'We certainly deny theology and should not be mealy-mouthed in so stating. We must fight organised Church fakirdom as we fight organised labor fakirdom.. .'.[22] This letter from Twomey was in support of one from Frank P. Janke. He agreed with De Leon's reply to Connolly, except for the acceptance of religion as 'a private matter'. Challenging the Erfurt position, Janke argued that as 'Scientific Socialism is based upon the materialist conception of history' and as:

> theology or religion *denies* the materialist conception of history, and teaches that a divine being or power directs, or at least influences, the affairs of mankind . . . how can Comrade De Leon say

117

that the SLP does not concern itself with or attack theology, when at the very basis of scientific socialism we take our stand as against the teachings of theology, and we should not try to pass or smooth the question over.[23]

De Leon was anxious not to go down the road of explicit hostility to religion: Janke's point was only a secondary one, he insisted, the principal question being whether Connolly was right in accusing the *People* of attacking theology.[24] H. Eckstein stated the majority position on religion: 'As to Connolly, to the best of my knowledge, the party does not do as he claims. As to Janke, the party should not attack theology. Its phase is on the political field. What does Scientific Socialism care whether theology is scientifically wrong?'[25]

Connolly himself did not contribute to the correspondence, but not for want of trying. De Leon would not publish his letter, on the technical debating grounds that it raised new matter.Janke's letter expressed the view that it was 'entirely unfair' to deny Connolly space to answer questions put to him by De Leon: 'Don't ask a man questions which demand an answer and then deny him the means to answer them.'[26]

The June 1904 issue of the *Socialist* carried Connolly's reply to De Leon. It was ironic that the journal of the British SLP, whose members had previously had to write for the *People* because of the undemocratic editorial policy of *Justice*, was now having to be used by a member of the American SLP because of the restrictive editorial policy of the *People*. Far from rejecting the SLP, Connolly wrote that 'I consider the SLP of the US the clearest and most revolutionary of the Socialist parties in the world today.' Privately, Connolly had become disenchanted by De Leon: he wrote to his Scottish comrade, Matheson, that

I am convinced already that the game is not worth the candle. The candle being Dan's friendship. . . As to the question you ask

118

me about the previous crowdings out of the party, I am inclined to think that some few men *may* have been irritated at Dan's dogmatism and rather unscrupulous handling of their case.[27]

Whatever the extent of the personal animosities, De Leon retained faith in Connolly as a comrade, and during the winter of 1904 – 5 the latter was invited to lecture on several occasions in New York. In 1905 Connolly joined the IWW, working hard to build the movement in the area of Newark, New Jersey.

While in Newark Connolly made contact with the Italian Socialist Federation and attempted to win them for the SLP. He taught himself Italian and translated several articles from the Federation journal, *Il Proletario*, for the *People*. Realising, quite correctly, that an ethnic minority suffering the disadvantages of immigrant status, were ripe for the revolutionary movement, Connolly urged the SLP to make special efforts to relate to the organised Italian workers. The SLP already had its own Hungarian and Swedish-language federations, and subsequently the party even published one journal in a unique south Slavic language – one not even used by any capitalist state. Connolly's strategy was one of extending the policy of ethnic targetting which had already begun.

In January 1907 the New Jersey Section elected Connolly as its delegate on the NEC. In the same month, Connolly organised a meeting of Irish workers in New York to propose forming an Irish Socialist Federation. This led to a criticism being raised by a Swedish immigrant SLPer called Stromqvist, a close ally of De Leon's. In a letter to the *People* Stromqvist argued that ethnic federations should not be allowed in the SLP as they served only to divide workers. He had opposed the formation of the SLP's Swedish federation and now argued that socialists must 'tear down and remove all the artificial obstacles in the way of complete industrial and political unity of the

119

Workers of the World presented by the differences in Race, Color, Creed and Standards of living. . .'.[28]

Connolly replied by agreeing that ethnic federations within the SLP had no place and he would vote to abolish them. 'But', he wrote, 'as strongly as I am opposed to language branches in the party am I in favor of Race or Language Federations to organize all the sections of our heterogenous population.'[29] On 29 March the Irish Socialist Federation was formed, but neither it nor Connolly were to remain for long in the SLP.

The story of Connolly's departure from the SLP is one of those episodes in SLP history, not unlike the events of the Kangaroo split of 1899, in which De Leon and others seemed to be overtaken by constitutional delirium. The essence of the extraordinarily complicated dispute was that Connolly had moved a motion on the NEC stating 'that the NEC and its Sub-Committee have the right to insert official matter in the *People*'. The NEC Sub-Committee comprised members living in New York who administered the party's affairs in between the six-monthly NEC meetings. De Leon, who accepted that he, as editor, must make the *People* open to any statements sent in by the NEC, opposed providing the same right of access to the Sub-Committee. Connolly's motion was to give the Sub-Committee that constitutional right. When the motion was lost, Connolly contended that the NEC had voted away its control over the party journal. This was not the case: just because a motion is lost it does not mean that all propositions contained in it are rejected. There then followed a protracted saga in which New Jersey members wrote asking De Leon whether the NEC had relinquished its control of the *People*. De Leon denied that Connolly's motion stated what Connolly claimed it did, and stated that the true wording could not be settled until the Minutes of the last NEC meeting were adopted by the next one in six months' time. Frank Bohn, the National Secretary, supported Connolly's claim. In the midst of this public row – every tedious point was argued openly in the columns of the *People* – one Comrade Eck, a De Leon loyalist, attacked Connolly for calling De Leon 'A Pope'; and one Comrade Quinlan, a Connolly loyalist, complained that Eck had misquoted Connolly, who had, in fact, called De Leon 'a dictator'. After the blood-letting came resignations, foremost of which was that of Frank Bohn (who had signed the Industrial Unionist Manifesto in January 1905).

An example of the petty and mystifying nonsense which these squabbling revolutionaries presented to workers buying socialist literature is indicated by the following 'explanation' published in an article by Bohn :

> The words 'and its' (in the Olpp Minutes written '& its') were between 'NEC' and 'Sub-Committee'. The use of '&' for 'and' occurs repeatedly in the Minutes and once again in the portion photographed and printed in the *People*. It should be remembered that the document was written with a lead pencil. The bungler who erased the two words left a portion of the 't' (the top of the vertical stroke) untouched, and it shows plainly in the photograph. The period after NEC has been inserted. The 's' stood exactly in the present position, the word 'have' after 'Sub-Committee' clinches the case.[30]

One can imagine the weary worker, exhausted after a day's toil, excited to read the latest socialist literature and filled with hope for a co-operative society of the future, picking up this introspective nonsense and completely losing heart. De Leon 's willingness to indulge in such damaging internal feuding, and his inability to stop the SLP from tearing itself apart, indicates a weakness which seriously diminishes his role as one who could give direction to the socialist movement in its day-to-day activities.

Connolly's resignation from the SLP was not immediate. Indeed, he was appointed as a principal speaker at the party's 1907 may Day rally. In the same month he resigned from the NEC, with a view to standing again in order to obtain a vote of confidence. This resignation was not accepted; instead, the NEC decided to call a vote of all Sections on Connolly's recall from the NEC. Once recalled, Connolly was defeated by Eck in a by-election for the vacant NEC place. Shortly after this calculated humiliation, Connolly resigned from the SLP.

In June 1907 the dispute between Connolly and Frank Reed of the SLP was dragged into the IWW's *Industrial Union Bulletin*. Reed argued a version of the 'wage increases causes price increases' theory, and this was rightly refuted by a number of contributors, including J. P. Thompson, Pat Quinlan and E. Baer. On 26 October Connolly added his comments to the debate, pointing out that Marx had called the theory put by Reed 'an old, popular and wornout fallacy'. Two weeks later De Leon wrote to Rudolph Katz, an SLP member of the IWW's general Executive Board (GEB), asking Katz to write to Edwards, the *Bulletin*'s editor, proposing that De Leon reply to the 'wages and prices' debate. This seems an odd and somewhat vain way to intervene in a public correspondence, but could it have been the case that De Leon's wish to be *asked* to contribute was motivated by his uneasiness at, on the one hand, wishing to defend his SLP – STLA comrade, but on the other, realising that Reed's theoretical position was an utterly untenable one? Edwards did not invite De Leon to contribute. Instead, Trautmann wrote to De Leon complaining that the *People* had been publishing articles by one Markley attacking the IWW. De Leon, still hoping at this stage to remain within the IWW, did his best to pacify Trautmann. Unfortunately, De Leon's diplomatic style left something to be desired: he alleged that Trautmann's IWW secretary, Otto Justh, had joined a conspiracy led by Connolly to discredit the SLP.

On 22 December 1907 Connolly attended the GEB of the IWW with a proposition to incorporate 12,000 new York longshoremen into the IWW. At this stage, De Leon began proceedings against Connolly in the IWW. It is possible that he feared the entry of the Connolly-led longshoremen as a threat to the STLA's dominance in the Eastern IWW. Also, he doubted the effect that these 12,000 predominantly immigrant, Irish and Italian Catholic workers would have upon the level of class consciousness of the IWW. The increasingly syndicalist and anti-De Leonist IWW leadership had little interest in De Leon's charges against Connolly's 'false economics' and religious sympathies. The GEB refused to investigate the charges and it was left to De Leon, in the *People* of 29 February 1908, to accuse Connolly of trying to inject religious and racial questions into the IWW.

By the end of 1908 De Leon, as has been shown, was forced out of the IWW. James Connolly, despite his earlier 'complete' agreement with the SLP, joined the SPA. The Irish Socialist Federation published its own journal, the *Harp*, which was edited by Connolly. In it he argued that the IWW should form its own political party, so putting 'an end to all excuse for two Socialist parties'. 'Compromisers and schemers will still erect parties to serve their personal ends', wrote Connolly, 'but they will be deprived of their power to delude the real revolutionist by the simple fact of the existence of a political party of Socialists dominated by and resting upon the movement of the working class'.[31] Despite much personal bitterness towards the political character of De Leon, Connolly remained an industrial unionist and, in so far as his Marxism was not entirely superseded by nationalism, he continued to be an articulate defender of De Leon's conception of socialism.

Neither De Leon nor the SLP came out of the conflict with

Connolly with much credit. The dispute need not have developed with the intensity that it did. Katz's historical assessment of the conflict was that 'James Connolly wanted to become editor of the *Daily People* because he imagined himself to have been born to be an editor . . . 'and the job would provide him with an opportunity 'to demonstrate how a person can be a revolutionary Socialist and yet remain a good and pious son of Mother Church'.[32] It is a matter of historical dispute just how much of a Catholic believer Connolly was. De Leon appears to have held no religious beliefs, private or otherwise, although his wife Bertha did, and was an occasional church-goer. De Leon's vociferous hostility towards the Roman Catholic Church seems to have been inspired by the excommunication of the radical Father McGlynn on 8 July 1887 for supporting the Henry George Single Tax Scheme. De Leon editorialised frequently against the interference of Catholic priests and bishops in politics; he used the medieval term 'ultramontanism' to describe their papist ideology.[33] But the SLP could hardly complain about its members wishing to serve 'Mother Church' while at the same time admitting religious believers into its ranks. The SLP position seems to have been that religion was 'a private matter', but religious believers could enter the party only in a secondary status, not trusted with major political responsibilities. Connolly's positions on religion and morality were bound, eventually, to result in conflict with De Leon's essentially anti-religious, historical materialist outlook. At root, it was this intellectual incompatibility which made it inevitable that the two thinkers would part company.

7 De Leon's conception of socialism

What did De Leon mean by socialism? On the face of it, this seems to be a clear-cut question requiring a straightforward answer. Socialists are those who seek to establish a society of common ownership, democratic control and production for use, not profit. Indeed, that is what Daniel De Leon stood for; but generalisations do not constitute a revolutionary alternative. More questions need to be answered. By common ownership, do socialists mean nationalisation, that is, state ownership? De Leon regarded the state ownership of industries – what Bismarck had called 'State Socialism' when he carried out such a policy in Germany – as nothing to do with socialism. He wrote that 'there is as much Socialism in "State Socialism" as there would be drunkenness in "State prohibitionism", or protection in "State free trade".[1] When the SPA Congressman Victor Berger was called upon to explain to Congress what he meant by socialism, he propsed that 'Everything that is necessary for the life and development of the State, the State is to own and manage. There are certain business functions that the State will have to take care of. . .'[2] This would mean, said Berger, that the state would have to buy out the trusts, paying for them at their value. De Leon did not favour state management of capitalism, and neither did he advocate 'buying out' the capitalists. Socialism entailed confiscation, which he defined as 'the appropriation of property contrary to the laws of an existing social system'. In defence of the principle of revolutionary confiscation, De Leon cited 'the Revolutionary Fathers', who 'were asked: "Are you going to confiscate these colonies?"', to which 'no less a man than Jefferson answered the "confiscatory" charge: Whenever in the history of a people conditions become such that they have to be changed, changed they shall be. "Confiscation", from the British viewpoint, was the root of this republic . . . The question is, "Do the requirements of the working class demand a different state of society?" If the answer is "Yes", then that appropriation is not confiscation at all.'[3] By democratic control, do socialists mean that there will be no coercive state, or will there be a new kind of state to rule society? According to De Leon, 'We shall either have Socialism – and that means that the State shall have vanished, or we shall preserve the State, and then we shall have no Socialism.'[4] To many, including a number of 'socialists', this would sound like a description of an anarchist society. Does production for use mean solely for use, without any market or profit? Will money exist or not exist in a socialist society? How will incomes be allocated if the wages system has been abolished? No sooner are socialists called upon to answer these questions than it becomes clear that it is not enough simply to declare one's self for socialism.

Like most socialists, De Leon was fairly clear about what he was against. In January 1893, when the *Evening Wisconsin* accused socialists of being 'utopians' and 'dwellers mid rosy fogs', De Leon retorted that:

> Private ownership in the instruments of production – in the land, tools, machinery etc. – was at one time the basis of industry and of freedom; concentration of these instruments of production in the hands of a few, and the introduction of machinery establish a system of production upon so gigantic a scale that the individual small producer cannot hold his own; he is stripped of his instruments of production, and becomes a proletarian, a wage slave,

dependent for his existence upon the capitalist, who has concentrated in his own hands the things that are necessary for a living; this system fills the land with paupers, breeds crime, prostitution and sickness; freedom under such a system tends to disappear.[5]

The restoration of freedom demands the return of the instruments of production into common ownership.

This restoration was not seen by De Leon as being the outcome of a process of gradualism, either legislative or 'buying out' the capitalists. We have already seen that De Leon held a revolutionary theory of social transformation. The Socialist Industrial Unions (SIU) would not only provide the economic force required to support the political decision for socialism, but they would serve as the embryonic forms of post-revolutionary social organisation. As De Leon put it, 'the Industrial Union is, at once, the battering ram with which to pound down the fortress of capitalism, and the successor of the capitalist social structure itself'.[6]

De Leon's new social structure would be an industrial unionist administration. The most elaborate single account of it by De Leon is given in his 'Socialist Reconstruction of Society' speech of 1905 (originally entitled 'The Preamble of the IWW'). the structure of political parties makes them unfit to 'take and hold' the machinery of production because, under capitalism, the governmental system is territorially not industrially demarcated:

> Take Congress, for instance . . . The unity of the congressional representation is purely politically geographic... Congress – not being a central administration of the productive forces of the land, but the organized power of the capitalist class for oppression – *its* constituent bodies can have no trace of a purpose to administer production.[7]

Therefore, in the event of a socialist political victory, there

127

would be nothing for the elected socialist delegates to do except 'to adjourn themselves, on the spot, *sine die*. Their work would be done by disbanding. The political movement of labor that, in the event of triumph, would prolong its existence a second after triumph, would be a usurpation.'[8] The revolution accomplished, power must shift directly to the workers in their socialist industrial unions. Instead of geographical constituencies, throwing people together on the arbitrary basis of where they happen to live, 'The central administrative organ of the Socialist Republic . . . must be exclusively industrial.'[9] By 'industrial' De Leon did not mean that power would be confined solely to those workers in factories rather than those on farms or in offices. All those who work can join their respective industrial union. Eric Hass, a later editor of the *People* and advocate of the so-called 'SIU program', proposed the following categories for industrial unions: manufacture, mining, transportation, farming, lumber, food supply, construction and public service.[10] (In Tomkins's 1965 British version of the administrative scheme, he suggests textiles, food, manufacture, public services, mineralogy farming, building and chemicals as suitable categories.[11])

The locus of power in De Leon's plan for socialist administration would be the local workplace. Where one produces, rather than where one resides, would determine one's constituency. Industrial representation would involve workers electing their own foremen and managers locally, and also electing revocable delegates to represent the local SIU in broader based union bodies. So, within each industry representation would move outwards, from local SIUs to national ones, and between different industries joint administrative councils (or soviets) would be formed, culminating in a national General Executive Board of all the Socialist Industrial Unions. 'Where the General Executive Board of the Industrial Workers of the World will sit', proclaimed De Leon in 1905, 'there will be the nation's capital.'[12] In short, the workforce, organised into One Big Union of society's producers, shall be a self-administering unit, co-ordinating its needs and targets, beginning at the point of production.

De Leon may be credited with having tried to give positive consideration to the structure of decision-making in a non-capitalist society. No doubt his training as a constitutionalist enabled him to foresee some of the organisational problems which a classless and stateless society would present. Conscious of the alienated, imposed nature of the political state, which he recognised could operate only in a coercive and probably bureaucratic fashion, an attempt was made to locate power in a socialist society in the places where people would be closest to the economic power of the productive process.

It was an imaginative plan, but problems spring immediately to mind. What about members of society who do not work? Are the retired to have voting rights in the industrial unions? What about those who are in full-time study? What about children? None of the advocates of the SIU administration provide information about the status of those occupied as homekeepers. Will women who are pregnant or child-rearing constitute an industrial union? What about the disabled who cannot work?

Why should work be made the central focus of the new society? In a socialist society, the division which exists under capitalism between production and consumption may well be less distinct, if it exists at all. De Leon's decision-making structure can be accused of being somewhat economistic. Might it not be possible that once production begins to serve society rather than dominate it, the last place that people will seek to look in order to define their power will be in their identity as certain kinds of producers. Furthermore, it is doubtful whether inhabitants of a socialist society will wish to assume a single

129

productive role, either throughout their lives or, perhaps, for long enough periods to allow the industrial unions to serve as effective democratic bodies.

The SIU programme bears a striking resemblance to the utopian scheme for American social reorganisation depicted in Edward Bellamy's novel, *Looking Backward*. Of course, De Leon had, before joining the SLP, been a Nationalist, committed to the implementation of Bellamy's plans in the USA. It is quite clear, in examining De Leon's conception of socialism, that the profound influence of Bellamy did not leave him in 1890. This is made clearer than ever by reading De Leon's *Fifteen Questions About Socialism*, a pamphlet written in 1914 to defend the case for socialism against the criticisms raised by a Catholic journal, the Providence, Rhode Island, *Visitor*. De Leon acknowledges the influence of Bellamy, who advocated the organisation of the workers into a military disciplined 'industrial army':

> In his epoch-making work, *Looking Backward*, Edward Bellamy summed up the situation under Capitalism with the terse sentence, 'We go to war as an organized body, and we go to work like a mob'. The summary at once portrays the situation in the Co-operative Commonwealth . . . Every member thereof of 'military age', in the only war that civilized conditions will know, the War against Want, will be directly or indirectly productive.[13]

For Bellamy, the militarisation of labour was not a metaphorical proposition. In a summary of the social structure depicted in *Looking Backward*, Bellamy points out that the old economic problems:

> have been solved by the union of the entire nation in a general business partnership, in which every man and woman is an equal partner. The conduct of the industries, commerce and general business of the country is committed by the national firm to a so-called army of industry, which includes all the able-bodied citizens, men and women, between the ages of 21 and 45.[14]

In his *Fifteen Questions About Socialism*, De Leon suggests a period of compulsory industrial service between the ages of twenty-one and forty-two.[15] In Bellamy's summary, he writes of 'an invalid corps attached to the industrial army, in which the sickly and feeble . . . are enabled to undertake what they safely can for the Common Wealth'.[16] De Leon, answering a question about inherently unequal human abilities in a socialist society, drew a comparison between the organisation of labour in socialism and the German Army, which has its own section for the disabled. He observed that 'Co-operation upon the gigantic scale, now possible, finds a place for the "less favored", as the weak of sight, or otherwise unfit for military duty. . .'[17] Although De Leon himself cannot be held responsible for it, the *People* of March 1958 answered the question: 'How would retired workers, disabled adults and, say, widows with children, express their wishes and vote in a Socialist government based on the industries?', by stating that 'Obviously, in a Socialist democracy based on industrial representation, only those who work will be in a position to vote. At first blush this might seem to be undemocratic . . . – indeed, it might. To be sure, De Leon did not go as far as Bellamy with the 'industrial army' metaphor, but such a structure for decision-making is in danger of rendering powerless that section of the population who are, in a rigidly productive sense, non-workers.

De Leon also drew upon Bellamy's thinking in relation to his plan for income allocation in a socialist society. Like Bellamy, he did not envisage money as existing. But, also like Bellamy, he could not bring himself to envisage a system of moneyless, free access. De Leon conceived of payment in a socialist society being by labour-time vouchers. Marx had proposed a similar method of income allocation being necessary during the early, incomplete period of socialism, while economic scarcity still existed and free access could not yet be organised. De Leon's support for labour-time vouchers owes less to Marx's *Critique of the Gotha Programme* than to Bellamy's utopia. In *Looking Backward* incomes were equal, but the number of hours that had to be worked in order to obtain the vouchers would be determined by the number of volunteers for a particular job: the fewer the volunteers, the shorter the hours; the greater the surplus of volunteers over those required to do the job, the longer the hours. In short, incomes are equal in Bellamy's utopia, but hourly rates of compensation are unequal.

De Leon offered an illustration of his theory of socialist income determination which closely followed the economic reasoning of Bellamy: 'Say conductors and motormen are wanted on a new traction line. Say that there are 200 cars to be equipped. There will be wanted an equal number of each – 200 motormen and 200 conductors.' How would the hourly rate of compensation of these different types of workers be determined? The number of applicants for each of the jobs 'will be an exact index of the amount of tissue expended in each function. Temperamental and other exceptional causes being left aside, it will be found that the preference will generally be given by the applicants to the pleasanter, or easier, function, that is, to the function that consumes less tissue.' So, if 400 workers apply to be conductors, while only fifty wish to be motormen, 'it would follow that 1 hour of a motorman's function consumes as much tissue as do 8 hours of a conductor's'. This would mean that 'the motorman's 1 hour would receive a compensation equal to the conductor's 8 hours'. Such inequality in reward would motivate more people to want to be motormen, and this should lead to a more balanced adjustment in the rates of compensation of the two functions. But, if 'in the final adjustment 2 hours of the motorman's function are equal to 4 of the conductor's, then the voucher for labor performed – that is, for contribution made to the social store

– paid out to the motorman for 2 hours' work will enable him to draw from the social store as much wealth as the voucher paid out to the conductor for 4 hours' work'[18]

Having devised a 'socialist' system of wages – and that is what it is, even though De Leon does not refer to these unequal rates of compensation as wages – it became necessary to answer such questions as whether skilled workers will earn more than the unskilled; the indolent less than the industrious. De Leon answered that 'The income of the skilled worker, who loiters, will be less than the income of his unskilled fellow-worker who bestirs himself.'[19]

It is clear that, while De Leon stood for the abolition of the wages system, and deplored the wage-dependent status of the worker under capitalism (which he regarded as a kind of slave status), in a socialist society he envisaged the emergence of a new wages system. He would see it as being a fairer wages system than the capitalist one. Those who did not work would receive no income; those who toiled most, and undertook the least pleasant, most socially valued, jobs would have to work less for their income. That certainly seems more just than under capitalism, where it is those who do not need to work who receive the highest incomes. But, however just as an ideal, it is not compatible with the claim to have abolished wage labour. It would not end the clock-watching and time-counting which is traditionally associated with work under capitalism. It would not remove work from the status of employment, whereby it becomes a portion of the day in which one is not free, but has to sell oneself, perform work as a commoditised cost in the production process, struggle to make a living. In short, wage slavery will not have been abolished: labour-time voucher slavery would prevail.

De Leon's income theory, like his industrial administrating theory, is borrowed from Bellamy's utopia, where 'The lighter trades, prosecuted in the most agreeable circumstances, have... the longest hours, while an arduous trade, such as mining, has very short hours.'[20]

The limitation of access to wealth by an exchange mechanism based on labour-time vouchers means effectively that a new monetary system would be established in De Leon's socialist society. I have argued elsewhere that, while claiming to depict a moneyless society, Bellamy's utopia was, in reality, a monetary economy.[21] Likewise in the case of De Leon: he argued that 'Money is a necessary thing under a social system that produces for sale and not for use. . . Remove that and there is no money any more. Money vanishes absolutely. . .'[22] But what are labour-time vouchers, without which one is barred access to the common store of goods and services, if not money?

Bellamy's plan for social reorganisation (which he did not call socialism) was to be applied in one country: the USA. The movement which emerged to implement it was not coincidentally called Nationalism. This was partly an intellectual reflection of American conditions. Whilst it would be hard to envisage social transformation in one country alone in mainland Europe, where the close proximity of different populations and the economic interdependence of nations tended to compel socialists to speak of revolution at least in Europe-wide terms, the vastness of the USA, its material abundance and its distance from the rest of the world made visions of social revolution in one country more plausible. To a great extent,it was global ignorance rather than national arrogance which narrowed Bellamy's vision. Did de Leon conceive of socialism in one country? Apart from the fact that he was strongly influenced by Bellamy, there are other reasons for thinking that he did. De Leon's view that developments made social revolution possible in the USA more than in any 'other country under the sun', and that 'the storm center will be in the USA and not in Europe',[23] implies that he anticipated the establishment of American socialism before the rest of the advanced countries of the world had established it. This would mean that, for some time at least, socialism would exist in the USA amid a surrounding world of capitalism. Secondly, De Leon repeatedly referred to the 'Socialist Republic' or 'Industrial Republic'. By definition, a republic implies a national entity. Thirdly, the SLP in the years after De Leon's death has persistently spoken of the possibility, indeed likelihood, of socialism being established in one country: the USA. In 1904 De Leon was asked a direct question about the possibility of socialism in one country; he replied:

> It is not likely that all the countries of civilization will leap into Socialism abreast of one another. consequently, if there could be no Socialist country without all the others being Socialist AT THE SAME TIME, Socialism would have a poor show. . . One Socialist country, IF POWERFUL, would have the effect of rendering Capitalism untenable in the others. . ., if it is a weak country, the others would crush it. Hence we can see no prospect of the Socialist Republic starting anywhere except here in America. America alone, of all the nations, has both the inherent strength and the no less necessary strength of location.

The implication of this, to those familiar with the ideology of 'Socialism in One Country' in the 1930s, are worryingly clear. De Leon envisaged not only the paradox of socialism confined within the borders of a nation without a state, but also that this stateless country would be 'powerful' enough to overcome international capitalism.

De Leon was the product of his times, and his vision of the future was impaired by the fact that it was moulded too much in the technocratic and exchange-based values of turn-of-the-century USA. De Leon was too busy recruiting socialists – and

135

falling out with more than a few – to elaborate a conception of socialism nearly as coherent or valuable as his theories of capitalism and the means to destroy it. At least De Leon did try to offer some constructive ideas about the socialist future. He was well aware of the possible futility of doing so. He recalled the 'Tory pamphleteers who pestered [Washington] and the other Revolutionary Fathers with questions upon the kind of government they contemplated – was it to be a Venetian Doge affair, a Dutch Republic of high Mightinesses, or what? Washington's answer was: "First, lick the British". Similarly, he contended, socialist cannot 'give details in advance' about the nature of the socialist industrial administration, but must answer, 'First, lick the British of today'.[25]

In his 1894 Introduction to the translation of Kautsky's *Socialist Republic*, De Leon was clear about the dangers of revolutionary socialists devising blueprints for socialism:

> Few things are more childish than to demand of the Socialist that he draw a picture of the Commonwealth he labors for . . . Never yet in the history of mankind has it happened that a revolutionary party was able to foresee, let alone determine, what the forms would be of the new social order which it strove to usher in.

In the light of those words, perhaps it would be best to classify De Leon as a foremost revolutionary usher rather than a distinguished visionary of what William Morris called 'the change beyond the change'.

8 The last years and legacy of De Leon

Socialists tend to die frustrated or deluded: frustrated that human emancipation has not been achieved; or deluded that it has. De Leon entertained no illusion that socialist victory had been won. As time went on, especially after 1908, when the shining hope of the IWW ceased to glisten, De Leon began to recognise that, however urgently he advocated working-class revolution, the workers were to be a recalcitrant force, denying success to the SLP. As this frustrating fact became increasingly clearer to De Leon, he did not 'cease from mental fight'. Speech after speech, editorial after editorial, answer after answer in the *Daily People*'s 'Letter Box' column all testified to De Leon's undying commitment to the cause of revolutionary socialism. In his final six years De Leon persisted in supporting working-class militancy – such as the Paterson textile workers' strike which was initially organised by the Detroit IWW in 1912 and in which De Leon played a leading role – and exposing the futility of reformism. But, above all, the last years were devoted to expounding his own particular theory of revolution, which began to take the form of an unquestionable blueprint: Socialist Industrial Unionism.

It could be argued that as early as 1900 De Leon realised that the historical impact of the SLP was likely to be a limited one and that he either had to face up to being a big fish in a small pool, or, alternatively, learn to ingratiate himself with the possibilists, whose political soundness he could not trust.

This would account for his willingness to accept the principle of unity when it was proposed by the Second International, and his transparent eagerness to diminish the rift between the possibilists and himself at the formation of the IWW. However valid an interpretation that might be of De Leon's outlook in the early 1900s, there is strong evidence to suggest that by the end of his relationship with the Chicago IWW, frustration had pulled De Leon in directions which he would not have contemplated in earlier, more optimistic, times.

In February 1906 the states of Colorado and Idaho conspired to frame 'Big Bill Haywood, Charles Moyer and George Pettibone on a charge of murdering the notoriously reactionary Governor of Idaho, Frank Stennenberg. The three men were imprisoned unconstitutionally for eighteen months before the trial in which the prosecution's evidence collapsed. The arrest and prosecution was clearly an attempt to break the WFM by depriving it of its leaders. The IWW was also the target of this vicious frame-up. The persecution spurred a wave of protest. Factional divisions counted for nothing: indignantly united, the workers' watchword of the campaign was 'Shall Our Brothers Be Murdered?'. Mass meetings convened almost spontaneously: 50,000 workers marched through Chicago and 20,000 assembled on Boston Common on May Day 1907. De Leon threw his full weight behind the campaign to release the framed men. That they were not SLPers, and, indeed, were SPA men, caused no restraint in support. The day after Haywood, Moyer and Pettibone were arrested – or, more accurately, kidnapped by the state – an unequivocal campaign for their release was launched in the *Daily People*. For eighteen months De Leon persisted in editorialising against the men's imprisonment. This was all the more noticeable in the light of the conspicuous refusal of either the SPA or WFM leaderships to fight in any way for the release of their 'comrades'.

In November 1906 Haywood, from his prison cell, ran for governor of Colorado. In an unprecedented gesture of non-sectarian solidarity, the Colorado Section of the SLP was urged by De Leon to support the Haywood ticket. This is the only time ever that De Leon counselled the SLP members to vote for a non- SLP candidate; at any other time such compromising behaviour would have been regarded as a serious disciplinary offence.

In July 1907 Haywood was released. The clumsy capitalist state had, contrary to all its machiavellian intentions, created a working-class hero. De Leon was greatly impressed by the respect which Haywood had won. He realised that such charismatic appeal resulted not only from Haywood's near martyrdom and experience-backed oratorical talent but also from the fact that he was untainted by weighty ideological convictions. Haywood was the antithesis of De Leon, not because the two men's principles were very different but because De Leon had a reputation as a fiercely principled revolutionary ideologue, whereas Haywood was known as a revolutionary with no time for ideology. De Leon thought that it was a man like Haywood rather than himself who could build a mass socialist movement in the USA. Far from being arrogant and power-seeking, De Leon's political shrewdness in the isolated days of mid-1907 generated a degree of humility which led him to write to 'Big Bill', calling on him to lead the united socialist movement which he knew he could not develop himself. 'Things in America remain in a disturbed and disordered condition', wrote De Leon to Haywood on 3 August, but:

> it is a state of disorder and disturbance from which your acquittal is calculated to bring speedy order and harmony. . . We are again in the days when the old Republican party was organized out of warring free-soil and abolitionist, and of up to then wavering elements. Thanks to your own antecedants, your celebrated case,

139

the unanimity of the Working Class on your behalf, and your triumphant vindication, the capitalist class has hatched out the needed leader. The capitalist class has thrown the ball into your hands. You can kick it over the goal.

De Leon explicitly renounced any personal claim to such leadership: 'Those who have been early in the struggle have necessarily drawn upon themselves animosities . . . these animosities are unavoidable and . . . tend to disqualify such organizations and their spokesmen for the work of themselves speedily effecting unification. . .'. While rejecting the false claims that he controlled the SLP himself, De Leon pointed out that, if Haywood accepted the role offered to him, 'My individual efforts may be relied upon, if you desire them, towards the work that circumstances have combined to cut out for you.'[1] In short, he would do his best to persuade the SLP to merge into a Haywood-led movement. De Leon's effort failed utterly: Haywood did not even acknowledge the letter.

During the course of the Haywood–Moyer–Pettibone release campaign, in which SLP and SPA members worked together single-mindedly, a desire for unity began to spread through the rank and role of both parties. If they could form an effective united front to fight against state injustice, why not do the same in the struggle for socialist justice? This was not a new question in 1907; some members of both parties had long regretted the 1899 split in the socialist movement of the USA, and the desire to heal the rift became greater when the IWW was formed. On 11 December 1905 Eugene Debs and Daniel De Leon shared the platform before a mass meeting held in the Grand Central Palace, one of the largest meeting halls in New York City. If socialist speakers could unite on one platform, then so could less prominent socialists in their local branches, reasoned many rank-and-file members. In the same months as the Debs – De Leon meeting, a unity conference, initiated by the New Jersey section of the SPA, took place. Other such conferences were held in other states. Political unity between the SLP and the SPA Leftists was apparent, but formal unity did not occur because, when state polls were held, the SPA members refused to commit themselves fully to an industrial unionist strategy, fearing that this would alienate the socialist movement from the AFL.

In January 1908 unity was again placed on the SLP agenda. Boris Reinstein, an NEC member from Erie County, Buffalo, New York, proposed a resolution advocating unity talks with the SPA. Two factors made the NEC agreeable to the idea: the recent campaign in which members of the two parties had worked as comrades; and the previous year's resolution by the Stuttgart Congress of the Second International which called for socialist unity where there was more than one socialist party in any nation. De Leon supported the unity resolution. Having failed in his appeal to Haywood, he knew that now he must do what in previous years would have been unthinkable, namely attempt to negotiate a merger with the long-detested Kangaroos.

On 21 February 1908 De Leon made an unprecedented move. He delivered a speech in the New Pythagoras Hall in New York City not on behalf of the SLP, but 'simply as one of the many people active in the Socialist Movement, and merely exercising the right of thought and speech'. The speech conveyed the tone of one who was not enthused by the prospect of unity, but historically conscious enough to realise that only on the basis of unity could the growth of an American Socialist Party be seriously anticipated. Such unity, argued De Leon, would need to replicate the broad alliance of socialists of different outlooks upon which the Second International was based: 'The theory of the International Congress regarding the "Socialist Family" established the broad basis of concerted action.' And, dramatically sweeping aside his fundamental commitment to a party of impossibilist purity, De Leon spoke approvingly of how 'The International Congress takes in the "Mountain" and the "Vale", leaving to time to demonstrate whether the "impossibilist" "Mountain" of to-day, or the "possibilist" Vale is to be the force of tomorrow.' Such possibilist – impossibilist co-existence 'points the way for the same application in America'.[2]

The motives for De Leon's 'Unity' speech are explicable, but the magnitude of the strategic volte-face leaves one wondering quite how De Leon could seriously have envisaged unity working. How could those who, as a matter of principle, rejected all minimum reform demands be allied with unashamed reformists? How could those who regarded the AFL as a main bulwark of capitalism unite with the 'labor fakirs' they had spent years attacking? How could the highly centralised and disciplined members of the SLP form a coalition with socialists who regarded state sectional autonomy as an organisational right, and could not even publish a national newspaper? The whole project was a fantasy – perhaps evidence that delusion and frustration are closer sentiments than one might at first think. Henry Kuhn used his NEC position vigorously to oppose the unity talk coming from De Leon and Reinstein. In the event, the minority opposition to unity in the SLP did not matter; it was the SPA, which in 1908 was to make a remarkable electoral impact with 420,793 votes cast for Debs, which felt sufficiently confident to dismiss the SLP's advance. Five years later it was Debs, by then disgusted by the possibilist – gradualist leaders of the SPA whom he called the 'Slowcialists', who urged unity between the SPA Left and the SLP.[3] Between 1908 and 1910 De Leon supported all unity moves, but after the attempt by the SPA to remove him from the Copenhagen Congress of the Second International (see

Chapter 4), he appears to have lost patience with his old rivals, accepting the principled requirement for the SLP to go it alone. When the SPA organised a speaking tour in 1910 for the German 'revolutionary socialist', Karl Liebknecht, De Leon met him for three hours in Newark, New Jersey. Liebknecht put it to De Leon that it was tactically expedient for the revolutionary minority to join the bigger, reformist SPA. De Leon was left unimpressed by such reasoning.

As well as De Leon's 'Unity' speech, 1908 saw another unprecedented event in SLP history: a convicted murderer, Morrie Preston, was nominated as the party's Presidential candidate. Preston was an SLP member and IWW organiser in Nevada. Although he was a miner, he supported the picket against a restaurant owner called Silva, who had badly treated a waitress and caused a strike.Silva responded to the picket line by pulling out a gun; Preston responded by drawing his own gun and shooting Silva dead. For De Leon, the defence of Preston involved more than just one man's wrongful imprisonment:

> Preston was exercising a civic right when on picket and assaulted. More than that – no picket duty, no strike; no strike or boycott, no union; no union, no co-operative or industrial republic is attainable. Thus the whole labor or socialist movement may be said to be pivoted upon the vindication, or the crushing, of Preston.[4]

De Leon's persistent concern to defend the constitutional right of the people to bear arms is a good example of his peculiar Americanism. He complained when the New York gun laws were reformed in 1911:

> It should be a right of the citizen himself to elect whether to bear a pistol, a small arm, that can be commodiously carried, or to burden himself with a shotgun. . . to render the 'possession' of

such firearms a misdemeanour, unless with the consent of government, is practically to disarm the people.[5]

De Leon sought popular support for Preston, perhaps hoping to sustain the feeling of the Haywood release campaign. Once again, the effort resulted in disappointment. Preston took his lawyer's advice and declined the Presidential nomination. In the 1908 election the SLP candidates (August Gillhaus of New York and Donald Munro of Virginia) obtained a mere 14,018 votes, 0.09 per cent of the votes cast. This was the SLP's lowest poll ever.

By the second decade of the century De Leon, although only in his late fifties, appeared to be an old man. He was short: five feet five inches in height, but was solid and muscular. His moustache and long beard were grey, and his piercing grey eyes conveyed the sagacity of a veteran in the world of ideas. De Leon tended to move slowly, often using a stick. Even in his forties he was known by his comrades as 'the old man'. His life had been free of the worst extremes of poverty, but he never had much money and his income as editor of the *People* was often unpaid. As a lecturer at Columbia University he had been paid $20 per lecture for twenty lectures a term. When he became editor of the *People* he was paid $12 a week; this rose to $30 by the time of his death, but when he died the SLP owed him $3,500 in salary arrears. His friend, Olive Johnson, remarked that De Leon 'lived very plainly and simply', but was not 'one of the class of "intellectuals" who go about and make a virtue and a fashion of poverty'.[6] He was a dedicated family man, and especially enjoyed his periods of summer relaxation in rural Connecticut. Bertha De Leon recalled that her husband had never allowed himself to become totally preoccupied with political life, 'and he was as much interested in the first tooth of the baby or the newest word spoken by the toddler, or the newest bird's nest discovered by the older ones as though the momentous social problems had never existed'.[7] But it was hard for one who had given so much of himself to the SLP ever really to escape from it; even in the last few years, when the symptoms of heart disease aged him faster than ever, De Leon continued a vigorous work routine.

They were frustrating years. De Leon had predicted that the USA was on the brink of revolution as far back as 1896, when he spoke of those who could 'comprehend the situation of our country – that there is a popular tidal wave coming' and predicted that 'In the crash that is sure to come and is now just ahead of us, our steadfast Socialist organization will alone stand out intact above the ruins. . .'.[8] By 1902 the 'crash' had not come, but, in *Two Pages from Roman History*, De Leon declared that 'The capitalist class is on its last legs'.[9] Indeed, the penultimate passage of the SLP's Platform stated that:

> The time is fast coming when, in the natural course of social evolution, this system, through the destructive action of its failures and crises on the one hand, and the constructive tendencies of its trusts and other capitalistic combinations of the other hand, shall have worked out its own downfall.[10]

In part, all of this can be explained as having less to do with genuine historical expectation than with the ceaseless revolutionary need for a rhetoric of morale-boosting – in part. But there was an aspect of such prophetic talk which was rooted in the positivist certainties of dialectical evolution and historical inevitability, concepts which belonged to nineteenth-century Marxism and its claim to scientificity. The revolt against positivism which dominated the early twentieth century dismissed such processes as 'the natural course of social evolution' as obsolete clichés. In the spring of 1913 Charles H. Chase, an SLP member employed as a philosophy professor at Columbia

University, attempted to criticise the SLP on the basis of the anti-positivist vogue. He gave a lecture entitled 'Reconsideration of Socialist Principles in the Light of Henri Bergson's Philosophy'. Bergson had been a zealous philosophical crusader against the claims of social science. Chase's lecture was attacked in the *People* by Arnold Petersen. Chase, whom De Leon respected as a man of intellectual substance, responded with an article, the main purpose of which was to demonstrate the relativity of Marxist economic analysis, but which also, and more interestingly, criticised those socialists who saw socialism as an inevitability. Chase referred to two SLPers who had attended his lecture on Bergson and asserted that 'our doctrines are true, and since they are true, why, people have to come to us sooner or later'. Furthermore, stated these SLP members, 'when the world markets are eventually exhausted, as they inevitably will be, why, then the workers will have to establish Socialism'.[11] De Leon responded by repudiating such historical inevitabilism, pointing to 'the "human equation" in modern social evolution'. Material conditions which are ripe for socialism depend 'upon man to take evolution intelligently by the hand, and thus prevent social miscarriage. There is no fatalism, or millenial-attitudinism in a posture that implies confidence in the normal intelligence of our generation.'[12]

So, if De Leon died frustrated, it was not because he expected 'History' to have delivered the revolution to the workers, but because his confidence in the intelligence of the working class had not been reflected in their confidence in, or support for, the SLP. They had been bought off with reform. In a few of his last writings De Leon, while never advocating reforms, admitted that if these were the best changes on offer, they should be accepted. 'None minimizes, let alone denies, the value of reform where reform brings relief. . .' conceded De Leon, reporting a meeting of the Child Welfare League which was seeking legislation to abolish child factory labour.[13] De Leon's hostility to reform campaigns softened as he came to realise that the USA was closer to Europe than he had once believed: that an appetite for palliation is the most that could be immediately expected from the workers. Still, however, as late as 2 August 1913, De Leon wrote an editiorial rejecting entirely the need for 'an immediate demand platform':

> The overthrow of capitalism – that is a demand – it is THE demand – it belongs in the platform of a true political party of labor.
>
> Shorter hours – 10 instead of 12, or 8 instead of 10 – when really and ultimately the hours will be nearer to 3 than to 8; higher wages, which means less exploitation, when really and ultimately wageism is to be abolished; a minimum of sanitary ventilation in factories, when really and ultimately the factory is to cease being a hole and is to become a parlor; these and the like are not 'demands'. They are intermediary stepping stones, to be discarded as soon as possible in the onward March. They have no place in the platform.[14]

Until the end De Leon insisted that only conscious, political action of a revolutionary nature could transform society. Reforms would never lead to socialism and neither would the new system evolve automatically. As early as 1908, 'in the *A s To Politics* debate, De Leon envisaged one other historical scenario. Capitalism could become more dominated by monopolies, and the workers could fall further still under the ideological domination of pro-capitalist union leaders and reformist politicians until a new system, which De Leon called 'plutocratic feudalism', would emerge. Under such a social order 'the many will sink to the depths of serfs, actual serfs of a plutocratic feudal glebe'.[15] De Leon seemed to have in mind here a vision of totalitarian monopoly, not unlike that which did later emerge under the Fascist corporate state and Stalinist state capitalism.

147

From early 1914 De Leon did not appear in the SLP offices, then at 28 City Hall Place, New York City. He had his last ever *People* editorial published on 7 February. He spent much of the time in his final months preparing notes for a lecture on the American satirical humourist Armetus Ward, whose writings had for long provided his favourite reading matter. The *People* published regular reports on his declining health. De Leon's physician was SLP-member Julius Hammer, the father of Armand Hammer, the millionaire owner of Occidental Petroleum, who repeated in his autobiography the common notion that De Leon was a fanatic, claiming that he had 'effectively brainwashed' his father! On 11 May 1914 De Leon's weak heart stopped beating. The obituary in the *People* noted that

> In losing him we lose a man whose very life was dedicated to the emancipation of the working class from wage slavery. . . When the history of the labor movement and the Social Revolution will be written by future historians, his name will be mentioned with reverence as one who gave of the fullness of his truly wonderful mind and heart that the Disinherited of the earth might come into their own.[16]

Few beyond the insular ranks of the SLP had much good to say about De Leon while he lived. When he died both the left-wing press and the capitalist newspapers paid tribute to him. (The venomous obituary in the *Volkszeitung*, quoted in Chapter 1, was an extraordinary assault.) The SPA's *New York Call* commented that.

> In a movement which recognizes the mockery of hero worship his name is great. No eulogy was ever stronger than this. . . There are few orators in America who can sway an audience as Daniel De Leon could. There are fewer who would refuse the temptations to do so as Daniel De Leon often did. . . To get the exact idea in is mind to as many in the audience or among his readers

who were capable of getting all seemed to be his dominant ambitions. . .; through it all there stands out very clearly the memory of a great educator and a truly great man.[17]

The *Newark Evening News* observed that:

when three thousand people gather in a public building to attend a funeral service and half a dozen leaders of a great organization eulogize the life and work of the deceased; when fifty thousand line the streets in prayer, it is evident that someone with an unusual personality has died.[18]

It is customary for biographies to conclude with a summary of the practical achievements of their subjects. In the case of De Leon a summary of failure would be more appropriate. De Leon did not succeed in destroying, or even slightly denting, the edifice of American capitalism.

The failure of American socialism to be taken up by the workers was far from being a political problem unique to De Leon. It seemed, at the turn of the century, as if the USA was the model of a successful capitalist society. In posing the question, *Why is There No Socialism in the United States* in a series of articles in the *German Archiv fur Sozialwissenschaft und Sozialpolitik* in 1905, Werner Sombart concluded that the relative material prosperity of the American workers had created in them a resistance to socialist ideas; the average worker in the USA had been turned into a 'sober, calculating businessman without ideals' and amongst such people 'all socialist utopias come to nothing on roast beef and apple pie'. Between 1870 and 1900 the American gross national product had tripled, while many workers saw a rise in their real wages and most were better off than their European counterparts. The *New York Tribune* of 7 February 1894 could report a Police Department survey which found 206,701 people living in New York

City without any means of support, but in general, American capitalism projected itself as reflecting the successes of social mobility and political democracy. The two major capitalist parties managed, as they do to this day, to stay clear of class ideology and to pander to those who aspire to prosper as beneficiaries of 'the American Dream'. Unlike in Europe, where the movement for socialism grew up alongside the emergence of trade unions which often embraced a militant awareness of working-class exploitation, and where workers had actually experienced participation in the revolutionary tradition as they aided the capitalists in their struggles against feudal forces, in the USA class politics were regarded as being antithetical to the ideal, shared by political leaders of both parties, that *post-bellum* American society could be peacefully inhabited by free and equal citizens. This was a huge belief to shatter, and De Leon was not to be blamed for the fact that those who must be discontented for socialism to be on the agenda were, on the whole, economically complacent and politically settled, if not entrenched.

The AFL, which De Leon devoted years to displacing, was numerically bigger and more powerful in 1914 than it had been in 1890; the Knights of Labor, which he tried vainly to win as a force for socialism, was defunct by 1914; the IWW, in which he invested such energy and hope, had failed by the time of De Leon's death to muster more than a very small minority of workers to its anarcho-syndicalist cause; and the Second International, in which De Leon saw all of the possibilist inadequacies of European social democracy, was to commit a most appalling betrayal of working-class interests when world war broke out three months after his death. The Detroit IWW, which in 1913 became the Workers International Industrial Union, failed miserably to reflect the dynamism or popularity of the original Wobblies, and was quietly disbanded by the SLP's Convention in 1924. The SLP, to which De Leon devoted himself unsparingly between 1890 and 1914, did not become a major force in American politics. Its size was not significantly greater when he died than when he joined. Its vote in Presidential elections increased from 21,163 in 1892 to 29,374 in 1912: a percentage increase of 0.02 from the total votes cast. De Leon himself had stood as an SLP candidate for political office on several occasions, never once winning an election or even coming close to doing so. In 1891 and 1892 he ran unsuccessfully as governor of New York. In 1896 De Leon was the SLP candidate for Congress in the 9th Congressional District of Manhattan and polled 4,300 votes. More frequently he stood for the 16th Assembly District of Manhattan in the New York City municipal elections. In 1897 De Leon won 1,854 votes, beating the Republican candidate into third place by 400 votes. In 1898 this increased to 2,207 votes; this was the year of the SLP's peak national vote (in all local elections combined) of 82,204. In 1899, following the tremendous upset of the SLP split, mainly centred in New York City, De Leon won 2,000 votes. This followed an outrageous campaign of vilification against De Leon in which leaflets were distributed by 'Kangaroos' which denounced him in every conceivable manner – including the allegation that he was a police spy and an agent for Bismarck! Nearly every one of De Leon's closest comrades in the SLP – Vogt, Sanial, Bohn, Ebert, 'Mother' Bloor, Connolly – deserted him before his death, often turning with intense acrimony against him. De Leon certainly did not succeed in impressing his socialist vision or strategy upon the vast majority of the American population, most of whom were completely unreached by the SLP, De Leon or any kind of revolutionary socialist propaganda.

De Leon's principal achievement was his unequalled intellect as probably the most knowledgeable and creative American

Marxist in a political culture which has tended to resist theory of any kind, and particularly non-pragmatic socialist theory. What Weydemeyer and Sorge had carried over from Germany as an ideological implantation upon foreign soil, mainly for immigrant consumption, De Leon established as an intellectually impressive tradition of American Marxism. The achievement consisted of not simply nurturing such an intellect (for, as Marx said, the point is not to interpret, but to change the world), but of the fact that De Leon's influence upon others has ensured that his ideas have endured.

Like most matters concerning De Leon, the extent and value of his influence on those who came after him is riddled with complications. For example, it has been frequently asserted, by Leninists as well as De Leonists, that Lenin's Bolshevism was strongly influenced by De Leon. This claim, which we shall examine, could be false, in which case De Leon's influence upon world history has been grossly exaggerated; or it could be true, so lending weight to the depiction of De Leon as an embryonic Bolshevik.If De Leon was a pre-1917 Leninist does that enhance or diminish his Marxist credentials? A similar question regarding De Leon's influence poses itself when one looks at the post-1914 history of the SLP. A biography of this nature is no place to attempt an historical consideration of over seven decades of the post-De Leon SLP, but even in this brief account of the SLP after De Leon, it will become clear that one must decide whether the party has evolved as it has by faithfully following the path determined by De Leon or by betraying it. And if the SLP's 'Marxist-De Leonism' is the apt culmination of De Leon's influence, are we to conclude that De Leon has inspired a fighting socialist movement or an intolerant, dogmatic sect?

There are other examples of De Leon's influence which are less difficult to interpret. Eugene Debs was clearly influenced by De Leon. In 1912 he wrote in J. A. Wayland's journal, the *Appeal to Reason*, that:

> It is foolish to say that the Socialist Labor Party is dead. It is not dead, and for my part I do not want to see it die. . . Many of my early lessons in economics were taught me by that little 'bunch of fanatics', and I am not the least ashamed to admit it. . . I can never forget that little band of valiant comrades – frenzied fanatics if you please, but still of the stuff of which revolutions are made. For years they were a mere handful, and yet they fought as if they had legions behind them. . . There are not many of them, but few as they are, they have the backbone to stand alone. There are no trimmers or traders among them.[19]

This was no patronising obituary. Debs wrote these words in the year that he stood as the SPA's Presidential candidate in the face of the bitter opposition of his party's increasingly reactionary right wing which mistrusted Debs as an impossibilist. In the *National Ripsaw*, which he edited, Debs declared that 'we believe the Socialist Labor Party to be right' because it does not 'compromise for the purpose of currying favour with craft-union officials. . .'. 'Industrial organization is the foundation of the revolutionary movement'. wrote Debs, 'and without such organization political action is in vain and industrial democracy remains a dream.'[20] This was the De Leonist position, not that of the SPA, to which Debs belonged. In 1913 Debs sought in vain to obtain unity between the two parties on the basis of De Leon's Socialist Industrial Unionism. De Leon, in one of his final writings, acknowledged that it was 'hard to tell Debs from the SLP so far as the union question was concerned'.[21] Had Debs, whose charismatic popularity was the converse of De Leon's status, joined the SLP or a merged party, it is interesting to speculate how much more impact De Leon's ideas might have had.

Like Debs, who was no theoretician, Joseph Schlossberg, the

leader of the Amalgamated Clothing Workers union, owed his political education to De Leon. Schlossberg's union represented some of the most highly exploited workers in the USA, and the SLP was active in the union's campaign against the starvation wages being paid by the New York sweatshop owners. Speaking in this campaign was one of De Leon's final activities before his illness. Chapter 17 of Schlossberg's book, *The Workers and their World* is devoted to 'Daniel De Leon – the Pathfinder'. 'Daniel De Leon was the supreme intellectual figure of American socialism', he wrote. 'My gaze is fixed firmly upon socialism as the ultimate goal of the labor movement. I see no other hope. I have received my labor movement schooling under the rigid schoolmastership of De Leon.'[22] He was not alone. Most of the people who founded the Communist Party of the USA in 1920 had, at some time in their political evolutions, been politically educated by De Leon. Indeed, without the legacy of De Leon it is difficult to think of any source for Marxist education in the USA, apart from the minutely small Socialist Party of the United States, an SPGB-linked impossibilist party formed as a breakaway from the Detroit SPA in 1916. (The SPUS later became The Workers Socialist Party, the Socialist Educational Society and, eventually, the World Socialist Party of the US, which still exists.[23]

Small De Leonist bodies emerged in Canada and Australia, in both countries related to the international spread of the IWW. The most significant De Leonist party outside the USA was the British SLP, the origins of which were considered in Chapter 6. In addition to the writings of the English impossibilist, William Morris, the works of De Leon provided the chief intellectual sustenance to the revolutionary minority which left the SDF in 1903–4. In two key respects, however, the British SLP was not a De Leonist party in the same sense that the American SLP was: first, it did not abandon a minimum, reform programme; and secondly, it did not promote a policy of dual unionism.

The inaugural conference of the British SLP, held in Edinburgh in June 1903 – three years after the important Tenth Convention of the American SLP – adopted a reform programme for the new party. The *Socialist* of April 1906 made clear that 'the SLP recognises . . . that by whatever measures the workers may be able, even temporarily and in a small degree, to resist the inevitably increasing powers of exploitation of their masters, such measures have the full and wholehearted support of the SLP.' This did not meet with the agreement of all SLP members: the Edinburgh branch tried from the outset to remove this possibilist deviation from the SLP's programme. Their attempt at the Second National Conference in 1904 succeeded in gaining support from half of the delegates voting, but still the British SLP retained its reform policies. The degree to which these were emphasised differed from branch to branch, depending on the impossibilist tendencies which existed within them. For example, when Thomas Clark was put up as candidate in the 1903 Glasgow municipal election, his manifesto announced that 'all we can expect to do is to ease the pressure of wage slavery, pending the entire overthrow of capitalism'.As measures promised 'to brighten the existence of the army of toilers', Clark's manifesto offered cheaper council house rents, a minimum wage for council employees, free school meals and public works programmes to provide jobs for the unemployed. When the more impossibilist-inclined Falkirk branch put up William Gibson as its candidate in the 1904 municipal election, their manifesto declared that 'If returned to the Town Council our candidate will endeavour to support any measures that are calculated to benefit the workers. But we desire to impress upon you the fact that it is entirely beyond the power of any palliative legislation to do more than slightly ease the hardships of the oppressed class.' Unlike the Glasgow manifesto, which sought votes on the basis of workers' appetites for immediate, temporary relief, the Falkirk one insisted that:

> We . . . desire no man to vote for our candidate unless he is in full agreement with the principles, policy and programme of the Socialist Labour Party. . . Those who are not fully in accord with our principles, who are not prepared to work along with us for the . . . establishment of the Socialist Republic, are respectfully invited to use their vote in whatever fashion their wayward fancies suggest, but on no count to cast it for him. [i.e. Gibson of the SLP].

De Leon did not intervene in the British SLP's debate on reforms, perhaps thinking that, like elsewhere in Europe, it was necessary to accept reform policies from socialists in 'politically backward' Britain. In fact, the British party that was closest to the anti-palliative position of the American SLP was the Socialist Party of Great Britain (SPGB), which opposed the British SLP partly on a tactical question arising from the process of seceding from the SDF, but, more substantially, on the issue of the minimum programme. The SPGB's position was that 'Our members oppose no reform which benefits the working class. We, however, resolutely decline to barter our Socialism for some vague promise of reform that resembles the proverbial pie crust. . . Further, practically the whole of the so-called "reforms" at present proposed would not, under present class rule and economic conditions, materially benefit the workers if obtained.'[24] This was De Leon's position, although, ironically, the accepted De Leonist party, based mainly in Scotland, was openly hostile to the SPGB position.

On the trade union question, the British SLP found itself in very different conditions from those existing in the USA. British trade unions were relatively strong compared with the AFL. Trade unionism had a much longer history and firmer tradition in Britain than in the USA. For the British SLP to have advocated dual unionism would have been politically suicidal. Yet, if they wanted to imitate the De Leonist line, then rejection of the 'pure and simple' unions was imperative. In an effort to draw a line of compromise, the British SLP's trade union policy was unclear. In 1903 the British SLP avoided all mention of a trade union policy in its *Manifesto to the Working Class*. Then, in February 1904 dual unionism was advocated, proposing that socilists should form union bodies in order to conduct 'skirmishing operations with the view to seizing small points of vantage' on the industrial field.[25] After this the British SLP adopted the American SLP's 1900 position of refusing members the right to hold office in a non-socialist union. Most British SLP members simply ignored such a rule. How could they accept office only in socialist unions when none existed? At least De Leon could urge his members to join the STLA; in Scotland there was no STLA. When the IWW was formed, the national Executive Committee of the British SLP, without reference to the membership, echoed De Leon's total support for the new movement. The NEC sent a resolution to the IWW hailing 'with unqualified approval' the formation of the IWW and promising 'to work incessantly for the formation and success of the British wing of that movement in place of the so-called Trades Unions, based as they are on capitalist principles'.

The NEC's endorsement of the IWW did not satisfy all members of the British SLP. A number of Glasgow members (including Tom Bell and Richard Dalgish) resigned from the party, issuing a leaflet entitled *The Decadence of the Socialist Labor Party*. The statement accused the NEC of acting undemocratically, and complained about the American SLP's support for Haywood in the Colorado election for governor, contrary to the constitutional prohibition on the SLP supporting non-party candidates. Most importantly, the authors of the leaflet opposed the IWW principle of the economic movement dominating the political wing. They accepted the STLA model for socialist unions, with the British SLP controlling such a body. Their two objections to the endorsement of the IWW were: firstly, that the British SLP was far too weak in Britain to attempt to initiate dual unions; and, secondly, that the politically hybrid nature of the membership of the IWW would lead to the class-conscious SLP playing a secondary role to the predominantly non-class-conscious IWW. In their view, 'The political movement is the forerunner to the economic movement. They must be affiliated the one to the other , and the condition of membership must be of such a nature that they should have corresponding number of members, so that the one could not outstrip the other.'

At the British SLP's 1906 Conference in Edinburgh the majority endorsed De Leon's faith in the IWW. They decided to set up their own body, which, though too small to constitute an alternative union movement, would work within the existing unions putting the case for industrial unionism. In August 1907 the Advocates of Industrial Unionism (AIU) was formed in Birmingham.The AIU soon became dominated by non British SLP members and ideas. Its most enthusiastic organiser, E. J. B. Allen, who had begun political life in the industrial unionist minority of the SPGB and then joined the British SLP, pushed the AIU in a snydicalist direction, arguing that 'there can be no real working class political action' until the workers have been industrially organised.[26] What had happened to De Leon in the IWW, and what the authors of the Glasgow statement had warned in 1906, had happened. The British SLP, by quite unconstitutional means, managed to grab control of the ostensibly independent AIU and its press. E. J. B. Allen and a considerable number of AIU members left to form their own, syndicalist Industrial League. In 1909 the AIU resolved to become the Industrial Workers of Great Britain (IWGB). Despite a couple of militantly fought strikes, the most notable of which was at the Singer Sewing Machine Works in Kilbowie, the IWGB existed mainly as an industrial unionist fantasy – a model imitation of the American IWW. In 1913 the IWGB's general secretary, T. L. Smith, admitted that 'Even those that stuck with the IWGB have become dis-heartened with the non-success'.[27]

Despite its non-De Leonist position on reforms and its inability to adopt De Leon's industrial unionist tactics in British conditions, the British SLP did play a major role in spreading De Leon's writings across the most militant sections of the British working class. Most of the party's pamphlets consisted of translations of Marxist classics by De Leon or De Leon's own works. *Two Pages From Roman History* became an established classic within the labour movement, and when the worker-students of Ruskin College, Oxford rebelled in 1909 against the reactionary teaching to which they were subjected, it was De Leon's pamphlet which inspired the name for their new journal, *Plebs*, and the Plebs League, which was subsequently to play a key role in British working-class self-education. De Leon's 'What Means This Strike?' found its way into numerous workers' libraries – from mechanics' institutes to miners' lodges – and it would be no exaggeration to state that most of the trade union militants of the 1920s owed a considerable debt to De Leon for their education in Marxism. Indeed, cruel though the observation may seem, De Leon appears to have won more admiration from those who never met him or had organisational dealings with him than from the many who knew him better. In 1904 De Leon visited Britain for a lecture tour; this followed his attendance at the Amsterdam Congress of the Second International. His biggest meeting was held in the Free

Gardens Hall, Edinburgh on 21 August. A large crowd applauded his vigorous exposition of the basic principles of industrial unionism.[28] De Leon also addressed British SLP meetings in Falkirk and Glasgow, and one in Clerkenwell, London, at which SDF loyalists, led by Jim Connell, the author of *The Red Flag*, attempted to storm the platform and put an end to the impossibilist rally.[29]

It was after 1910, when the British SLP integrated itself most into the British labour movement, that it had its greatest success. In these years (1910 – 20) the party was less preoccupied with De Leon, impossibilism or any long-term objective than in building itself up as a left-wing leadership within the established trade unions. Several of the old De Leonists rejected this new policy, and one of them, R. McCraig, published a pamphlet entitled *The Decline and Fall of the SLP*, in which he asserted that 'the Party has been well-diluted ideologically by kowtowing to trade unionism'. In 1911 these De Leonist dissidents were expelled from the British SLP, and in June 1912 they established their own organisation, called the British Section of the International Socialist Labour Party with a journal called the *Proletariat*. After the Bolshevik revolution the British SLP split, with a large minority of its membership merging into the Communist Party of Great Britain in 1921. The majority continued as a dwindling De Leonist force with a few active members and little political impact. The party survived until the late 1960s, largely as a sort of revolutionary colonial appendage to the American SLP.

De Leon was acknowledged by others in Britain beyond the British SLP. Guy Aldred, the 'anti-parliamentarist' anarchist who stood three times for election to the House of Commons, regarded De Leon as 'the leading theorist in the Socialist Movement in America' and contended that 'his conception of social revolution . . . is the true and only conception'.[30] De

Leon would not have thanked Aldred for listing him as one of the pioneers of anti-parliamentry communism; presumably Aldred had not read *As To Politics*. De Leon's writings have influenced several leading figures on the British Left: to take just two examples, Aneurin Bevan recalled how his political education was gained when 'towards the end of the First World War, I became acquainted with the works of Eugene V. Debs and Daniel De Leon', which he discovered in the Tredegar Workmen's Library;[31] in 1958 Eric Heffer became quite taken by industrial unionism, 'its major exponent being Daniel De Leon'. Heffer wrote an article entitled 'The Case For Industrial Unionism'.[32]

In relation to events in Russia a far more ambitious claim has been made for De Leon's influence. This claim is to be found in the writings of Arnold Petersen, who, with character-istic overstatement in his assessment of De Leon, asserted that 'Lenin himself acknowledged the singular genius of De Leon, and hailed him Master Architect'.[33] On another occasion Petersen stated that 'Lenin devoted himself to a study of De Leon's works, recognizing . . . in De Leon a Marxist of the highest order and without a peer during the time that he worked in the socialist cause'.[34] These claims are not unique; they abound in SLP literature, and not only that written by Petersen. If true, they would demonstrate that De Leon's efforts to implement his socialist strategy were not without tangible effect; that after De Leon's death Lenin, whom De Leon had never acknowledged while still living, became a disci-ple of De Leon's and, therefore, in an indirect sense, the Bolshevik revolution and the state that it created could be seen as an expression of De Leonist influence.

Four references to comments by Lenin – a fifth was discov-ered in a book published in 1987 – have been used by De Leonists to support the claim in question. First, on 31 January

161

1918 the journalist, Arno Dosch-Fleurot reported in The *New York World* that:

> Daniel De Leon, the late head of the Socialist Labor Party of America, is playing, through his writings, an important part in the construction of a socialist state in Russia. The Bolshevik leaders are finding his ideas of an industrial state in advance of Karl Marx's theories.
>
> Lenin, closing his speech on the adoption of the Rights of Workers Bill in the Congress, showed the influence of De Leon, whose governmental construction, on the basis of industries, fits admirably into the Soviet construction of the state now forming in Russia. De Leon is really the first American socialist to affect European thought.

The second piece of evidence comes from John Reed, the author of *Ten Days That Shook The World*, who was acquainted with Lenin, and, upon his return from Russia, was reported by the *Weekly People* of 11 May 1918 as telling the NEC of the SLP that:

> Premier Lenin . . . is a great admirer of Daniel De Leon, considering him the greatest of modern socialists – the only one who has added anything to socialist thought since Marx. . . It is Lenin's opinion, Reed said, that the industrial state as conceived by De Leon will ultimately have to be the form of government in Russia.

Note that this is reported speech from Reed, not direct quotation.

Thirdly, in the *New York World* on 3 February 1919, Robert Minor reported an interview in which Lenin stated that:

> The American Daniel De Leon first formulated the idea of soviet government, which grew up on his idea. Future society will be organized along soviet lines. There will be soviet rather than geographical boundaries for nations. Industrial unionism is the basic thing. That is what we are building.

The fourth source is to be found in Arthur Ransome's *Six Weeks in Russia*, in which the author tells of a conversation with Lenin, who had apparently read an article in an English socialist journal comparing his ideas with De Leon's. The article in question was by William Paul, a founder member of the Communist Party of Great Britain and an ex-member of the British SLP. It had appeared in the *Workers' Dreadnought* in 1918. According to Ransome, after reading this article Lenin:

> borrowed some of De Leon's pamphlets from Reinstein (who belongs to the party which De Leon founded in America), read them for the first time, and was amazed to see how far and how early De Leon had pursued the same train of thought as the Russians. His theory that representation should be by industries, not by areas, was already the germ of the Soviet system. He remembered seeing De Leon at an International Conference. De Leon made no impression at all, a grey old man, quite unable to speak to such an audience; but evidently a much bigger man than he looked, since his pamphlets were written before the experience of the Russian Revolution of 1905. Some days afterwards I noticed that Lenin had introduced a few phrases of De Leon, as if to do honour to his memory, into the draft of the new programme of the Communist Party.

The most recent item of evidence is to be found in a book published in 1987 by the journalist George Seldes, who interviewed Lenin as late as November 1922. In fact, Seldes did not obtain any significant information from Lenin, but he was in close contact with Oscar Cesare, the cartoonist of the *New York Times* who spent many days sitting in Lenin's office sketching him. Seldes quotes Lenin telling Cesare that:

> Bolshevism, our reading of Marxism, actually originated in America. Daniel De Leon left the Socialist Party, he resigned, he founded a more radical party, a more truly Marxist party, which he called the Socialist Workers Party of America. What we have

done in Russia is accept the De Leon interpretation of Marxism, that is what the Bolsheviks adopted in 1917.

This account is clearly inaccurate historically: De Leon did not belong to the SPA and did not form the SWP, but joined the SLP which had already been going for fourteen years before his entry. None the less, the account is of particular interest because it suggests that Lenin was still acknowledging the De Leonist influence near the end of his life.,

Such evidence is not sufficient, however, to substantiate Petersen's claim that Lenin was profoundly influenced by De Leon. None of the accounts is reflected in Lenin's transcribed speeches. It is probable that much of what Lenin is reported as saying to American journalists was not initiated by him, but was a response to suggestive questions put to him: What do you think of the American socialists? How about the Marxist SLP? Have you come across De Leon? On the basis of hurried responses from Lenin – who was bombarded by journalists from many parts of the world at this time – and some over-stated reporting from journalists requiring a good American story, the myth of Lenin the De Leonist was born. It was also the case that Reed was anxious to woo the SLP towards the Comintern position, and this may have accounted for his flattering report of Lenin's admiration for De Leon.

Lenin certainly was aware of De Leon. In September 1915 the *People* expressed support for the anti-war Zimmerwald Manifesto, and when the Bolshevik, Alexandra Kollontai, visit-ed the USA that year with a brief from Lenin to make contact with anti-war Marxists, she visited the offices of the SLP and had a discussion with Arnold Petersen, the party's National Secretary.Kollontai obviously discussed the SLP's position with Lenin, who wrote to her in 1917 regretting that he lacked a full collection of SLP literature. At this time, when Lenin was categorising the 'socialist' parties of various countries into revolutionary and reformist wings, he made frequent references to the revolutionary stance of the SLP. He was uncertain about the SLP's attachment to the idea of the primacy of the economic movement and asked Kollontai to explain this to him. In February 1917 Leon Trotsky, who was living as an exile in New York, spoke at an SLP anti-war rally at the Cooper Union. None of this indicates knowledge of the SLP's De Leonist ideas, only of its existence as a revolutionary party. The sole comment from Lenin which is an exception to this came one month before the Bolshevik revolution, when he wrote of 'the American socialist Labor Party and its demand that "the political state give way to industrial democracy"'.[35]

Boris Reinstein, an SLP member, was in Russia at the time of the Bolshevik seizure of power. Reinstein probably did provide Lenin with De Leon's pamphlets. There is evidence that Lenin was impressed by at least one of these, for in the summer of 1920 he wrote to Bukharin that 'I think we should publish in Russian De Leon's *Two Pages* with Fraina's foreword and notes. I shall also write a few words'.[36] There is no record of a reply from Bukharin or of a Russian translation of *Two Pages from Roman History*. This could have been because the Comintern opposed giving credence to De Leon at a time when the SLP had declared the Bolshevik coup to have been a non-socialist revolution. In Lenin's *Left-Wing Communism — An Infantile Disorder* he refers to 'labor lieutenants of the capitalist class', calling this phrase 'the splendid and profoundly true expression of the followers of Daniel De Leon in America'.[37] But, contrary to Petersen's claim that Lenin had become a De Leonist, this phrase of De Leon's appeared in a chapter of the pamphlet entitled *Should Revolutionaries Work in Reactionary Trade Unions?*, in which his answer was precisely the opposite of the De Leon position. When, in August 1918, Lenin wrote his *Letter to the American Workers*, he mentioned his admiration of Debs, but made no mention of the SLP or of De Leon, who, according to Petersen, Lenin 'hailed' as the 'Master Architect'.

De Leon had no profound influence upon Lenin, although the latter clearly knew of De Leon and approved of some of his ideas. Also, the state developed in Russia by the Bolsheviks, bore some relation to the constitutional arrangement envisaged by De Leon. As was argued in Chapter 7, De Leon's industrial administration was largely borrowed from Bellamy's technocratic vision, so, to stretch the thesis further, one could argue that the American utopian, Edward Bellamy, was the first thinker to outline the form of the Bolshevik state. There is little of historical value to be gained in searching out such influences, and the most simple explanation for the Petersen claim is that it originated in a desire on the part of the SLP, which was overwhelmed by the events in Russia, to portray De Leon as a more influential historical figure than he was.

Regardless of the historical relationship, was there an intellectual similarity between De Leon and Lenin? The right-wing SPA leader, Morris Hillquit, said of De Leon that 'He was the perfect American prototype of Russian Bolshevism.' Such a claim was not intended as praise. Professor L. G. Raisky, the pro-Bolshevik historian from the University of Leningrad, who wrote admiringly of De Leon in 1932, concedes regretfully that De Leon was not in the Bolshevik mould:

> From the Bolsheviks De Leon was divided by his failure to understand the inevitability and necessity of a transitional epoch in the form of the dictatorship of the proletariat. He believed that the Socialist revolution would at once eliminate the State. . . We can thus see that no equation mark can be drawn between De Leon and Bolshevism.[38]

Who was closer to the truth, Hillquit or Raisky? To be sure, there were some crucial similarities between the political think-

166

ing of De Leon and the Bolsheviks. Both based their policies on the theory of class struggle. Both opposed the reformism of the social-democratic parties which dominated the Second International. Lenin, whose highly disciplined, centralised conception of the revolutionary party led to the split with the Mensheviks in 1903, was in many respects replicating De Leon's organisational principles. Lenin declared irreverence to legality and capitalist morality, as did De Leon in 1902, when he stated that 'Reverence for the usurper denotes mental, with resulting physical, subjection to usurpation.'[39]

Lenin held that the majority must be led to emancipation by the enlightened minority, the vanguard party. De Leon seemed at times not to hold that view. After all, the principle of industrial unionism was based on the need for a peaceful revolution backed by mass support; that was the central theme of De Leon's case in *As To Politics*. In *Socialism Versus Anarchism* De Leon argued that 'You must educate the masses first. . . You cannot move faster than the masses move with you in this twentieth century.'[40] This appears to be in line with Marx's dictum that 'the emancipation of the working classes must be the work of the workers themselves'. Other statements by De Leon exhibit a distinctly Leninist sense. In 'Reform or Revolution' De Leon makes the sound point that if the workers are 'not virile enough to strike an intelligent blow' for themselves, they are 'not fit for emancipation'. He proceeds to assert that 'while that is true, this other is true also: In all revolutionary movements, as in the storming of fortresses, the thing depends upon the head of the column – upon that minority that is so intense in its convictions, so soundly based on its principles, so determined in its action, that it carries the masses with it. . .'[41] The SLP's role was to be the head of the column of the American workers. Ten years later, at the Second convention of the IWW, De Leon's vanguardist attitude

167

became even more apparent. De Leon cited a criticism which had been made of the IWW's Preamble by someone who said that 'it was a mistake to attempt to organise *all* the workers'. De Leon responded:

> Ah, indeed, it is a mistake; only he did not carry his argument as far as I would have carried it. Not because you cannot organize all the workers, but because it is not *necessary* to organize all the workers. The revolutions of this world have been accomplished not by majorities but by minorities; only the minority had to be large enough and determined enough and convinced enough to *act*.[42]

In 1896 De Leon backed up his case for minority revolutionary action by citing the historical example of Pizzaro, who, with only a minority force, defeated the Incas. In 1906 he supported his position with reference to the struggle for American independence, pointing out that 'if a male vote or referendum had been taken, the colonies in this union would by a large majority have voted against independence. . . That revolution was accomplished by a clear-headed, determined minority.'[43] Lacking in both of De Leon's historical illustrations was a recognition that there is a fundamental difference between revolutions displacing one minority elite in order to establish another, and a socialist revolution aiming to abolish class power and dismantle the state. Lenin not only advocated minority action but also expected the vanguard to be composed mainly of intellectuals from outside the working class. De Leon seemed to come close to this view when he stated that 'The Labor Movement is entitled to, and needs all the knowledge of the age. Much of this knowledge cannot be the contribution of the proletariat.'[44] So, despite the exaggeration of the historical facts relating to De Leon's influence on Lenin, there is evidence to support Hillquit's suggestion that De Leon was something of an embryonic Leninist.

De Leon's most enduring institutional legacy is the SLP. On 22 February 1914 the *Daily People* was forced to become a weekly newspaper. De Leon, who was dying, wanted to sustain the daily, but the SLP's able accountant, Zimmerman, explained that the party was too small and sales too few to allow the venture to continue. Over seven decades later the *People* is still published – now fortnightly – and the SLP is still minutely small and without any significant political influence in the USA. Unlike the SPA, which has split in several directions since the days of Debs and, later, Norman Thomas, the SLP has continued an unbroken political tradition. That its failure has been so complete is an effect of a far greater phenomenon than itself: the much-discussed resistance of the American population to the ideas of socialism, and, more still, Marxism. But to what extent has the post-1914 SLP made good use of De Leon's ideas?

In the year of De Leon's death Arnold Petersen became the party's National Secretary. He did not leave office until 1969. Petersen, and the clique around him, dominated the SLP with extreme authoritarianism. Members, branches and whole state Sections were frequently disciplined for what came to be known as 'disruption', i.e. disagreeing with, or disobeying the leadership. De Leon stamped his authority upon the SLP because he was the party's most able and active thinker. That De Leon's comrades offered him such deferential respect created a tradition which was abused terribly by the less intellectually vivacious, sterile dogmatists who succeeded the De Leon role. In an internal SLP manual entitled *Disruption and Disrupters*, Petersen stated that its main purpose was:

> to put the newcomer in our movement on guard against disrupters and disruptive influences. . . Party history proves the essential one-ness of disrupters, and the uniformity of the course followed by all disruptions. When disruption rears its head, the loyal and well posted SLP man 'knows the answers' in advance.[45]

169

SLP members were taught to adopt ideological knee-jerk reactions to questioning, doubt or dissent, so much so that by the late 1960s many members felt intimidated and repelled by the doctrinaire sect in which they found themselves. In the resignations of those years, the SLP lost some of the finest De Leonists, including Eric Hass, who joined the SLP in the 1920s and was editor of the *People* from 1938 until 1967. In an article explaining his resignation, Hass wrote that 'SLP "democracy" is largely a myth. Authoritarianism permeates it, top to bottom.'[46] In his letter of resignation, dated 4 July 1967, Bruce Cameron pointed out that 'Both the authoritarian spirit and the [intellectual] stultification are the reason why the young stay away from the party in droves'. Since the late 1960s the SLP's membership has been falling. Some ex-SLPers formed new De Leonist groups; one of them, whose journal is the *Socialist Republic*, originated in a dispute between Petersen and some New York SLPers as far back as the mid-1920s. Critics of De Leon's disciplined party model may well see the fate of the post-1914 SLP as the inevitable culmination of his organisational principles. This would be unfair. The SLP over which De Leon presided was, in the main, a very democratic body: all officers were elected; internal minorities were given full opportunities to persuade the membership of their views, even in the party press. What the pre- and post-De Leon SLPs do have in common is an obsessive concern, occasionally bordering upon neurotic sectarianism, to guard against the reformist dilution of their principles. Perhaps that is the price to be paid by all small, revolutionary movements existing in an overwhelmingly non-revolutionary atmosphere.

The post-1914 SLP tended to turn De Leon into an infallible guide. While Stalinists were inventing the term 'Marxist-Leninism', the SLP devised 'Marxist-De Leonism', a term which it still uses to describe its ideology. As with all intellectual deifications, the creation of 'De Leonism' required followers to accept De Leon totally, rather than in part or in historical context. And the totality offered is one which has had to exclude those bits of De Leon's thinking which appear to contradict the essence of 'De Leonism'. For example, it was only after the widespread resignations from the SLP in the 1960s that Hass and others began to explore De Leon's sympathy for certain reform measures, whilst opposing reformism, as was shown in Chapter 4.

The post-1914 SLP has made a number of errors, most importantly concerning the nature of Russian society. Until 1939 the SLP regarded the USSR as an essentially progressive state which was carrying the socialist torch. At the time of the Moscow trials, Petersen praised Stalin's 'justice', comparing it with that of the SLP. This erroneous position arose partly from the mistaken belief that the Russian rulers were somehow under the influence of De Leon, and also from a dogmatic, unhistorical application of De Leon's theory that American socialists should not expect much from their European counterparts. To the credit of the post-Petesen SLP, the party has published a pamphlet admitting some of its past errors regarding the USSR.[47]

It should be clear by this stage that attempts to evaluate the significance of Daniel De Leon as a contributor to socialist thought are likely to be seriously clouded by long-standing caricatures of the man and his ideas. At one extreme there is the quite scurrilously defamatory novel, *Adversary in the House* by Irving Stone, which portrays De Leon as a crazed, power-lusting tyrant. For example, Stone has Debs visit De Leon's office to propose merger between their two parties (an incident which never occurred). De Leon responds:

Very well, Mr Debs, you come here to put yourself in my hands, and to lay your followers at my feet. I am willing to take in you and your organization, but you must understand the terms and conditions . . . You and your people come into my organization as obedient subjects. Your main task is to understand my will and carry out my orders.

Stone leaves Debs standing 'blinking, trying to understand the convulsions of De Leon's mind', and as he does so 'the man with the firm jaw and aggressive mouth' explains his unity conditions to Debs:

All new members were to be trained in De Leon's dialectics and utter no word except that which he had approved as the party line. Gene and his associates must empty their minds as completely as their bowels would be emptied by castor oil, then they would be given a new content by De Leon, one which they would never have to change, question or discard. They would all act as one, think as one, believe as one, do as one: and Daniel De Leon would be that One.[48]

Sadly, such rabid anti-Marxism, disguised as biographical fiction, has been followed by historians who have not taken the trouble to investigate who De Leon was or what he really stood for. At the other end of the spectrum of distortion are those hagiographical accounts written by Olive Johnson, Henry Kuhn, Arnold Petersen and Sam French (whose *Daniel De Leon – Immortal* must be read to be believed).

De Leon was far from being the strategic genius that his admirers depict him as, and he was nothing like the fanatical tyrant portrayed by his enemies. Above all, De Leon was a Marxist who refused to compromise and attend to the 'possible' within capitalism. He was an impossibilist, – if to stand for the abolition of capitalism and nothing less must be defined as seeking the impossible. He was second to none as a writer and speaker, providing the most logical of elementary introductions to socialist ideas; De Leon's basic writings should be required reading for all self-taught socialist thinkers. De Leon was all of that: he was also an inspiring optimist about history. As he proclaimed:

> the Party carries on its work of education encouraged by the knowledge that some day, somehow, something is bound to rip. And then, at that crisis, when the people who have allowed themselves to be misled from Mumbo Jumbo to Jumbo Mumbo, will be running around like chickens without heads, there will be one beacon light in the land burning as clear in that darkness as it is burning 'midst the clouds today; one beacon whose steady light will serve as guide; whose tried firmness will inspire confidence, and whose rockribbed sides will serve as a natural point of rally from which to save civilization.[49]

Notes

Chapter 1

1 Quoted in C. M. Rehmus and D. B. McLaughlin (eds), *Labour and American Politics* (Michigan, 1967), p. 138.

2 W. Haywood, *Bill Haywood's Book: Autobiography of William D. Haywood* (New York, 1929), pp. 183-4.

3 J. O'Neill, *Report to WFM Members*, 8 October 1906, pp. 5–6.

4 *Justice*, 11 April 1903.

5 *Justice*, May 1903, reprinted in the *Socialist*, June 1903.

6 *SLP Correspondence*, Wisconsin State Historical Society (WSHS), 26 September 1899.

7 See *Connolly–Matheson Correspondence*, National Library of Ireland (NLI), letters dated 30 January 1908, 1 March 1908 and 7 May 1908.

8 Quoted in A. Peterson, *Daniel De Leon – the Uncompromising*, p. 15.

9 M. Hillquit, *Loose Leaves From a Busy Life*, p. 183.

10 M. Dubofsky, *We Shall Be All – A History of the IWW*, p. 133.

11 B. Brommel, *Eugene V. Debs – Spokesman For Labor and Socialism*, p. 45.

12 S. H. Holbrook, *Dreamers of the American Dream*, p. 319.

13 D. M. Chewter, 'The History of the Socialist Labour Party of Great Britain from 1902 until 1921, with Special Reference to the Development of its Ideas', unpublished B.Litt. thesis, Oxford, 1965, p. 4.

14 B. W. Tuchman, *The Proud Tower*, p. 497.

15 R. Challinor, *The Origins of British Bolshevism*, p. 30.

16 H. Kuhn, 'Reminiscences of Daniel De Leon', p. 6.

17 Reprinted by the SLP as O. Johnson, *Daniel De Leon*, p. 8.

18 *New York World*, 15 May 1878.

19 B. C. De Leon, 'When First We Met', *Golden Jubilee of De Leonism* (Socialist Labor Party, SLP, 1940), pp. 10–11.

20 O. Johnson, *Daniel De Leon* (New York Labour News, NYLN, 1923), p. 11.[nlt]

21 De Leon, *Marxian Science and the Colleges* (NYLN, 1966), p. 66. from *Daily People*, 12 February 1904.

22 H. George, *Progress and Poverty* (New York, 1879), p. 200.

23 A. Petersen, *Daniel De Leon – Orator*, p. 11.

24 *New York Tribune*, 2 October 1886; cited in A. Petersen, *Daniel De Leon – From Reform to Revolution 1886-1936*, p. 8.

174

Chapter 2

1 D. Herreshoff, *The Origins of American Marxism: From the Transcendentalists to De Leon* (New York, 1973), p. 74.
2 S. Gompers, *Seventy Years of Life and Labor – An Autobiography* (New York, 1925), I, p. 55.
3 F. Engels, *Preface* to the American edition of *Condition of the Working Class in England in 1844*, 1887, in Marx–Engels, *Letters to Americans* (New York, 1953), p. 288.
4 *Proceedings of Tenth SLP Convention*, p. 97.
5 The *People*, 8 May 1898.
6 De Leon, *The Ballot and the Class Struggle*, p. 12.
7 The *People*, 6 December 1896.
8 *Proceedings of Tenth SLP Convention*, p. 7.
9 F. Engels, *Marx–Engels Selected Correspondence, 1846–95* (New York, 1934), p. 87.
10 The *People*, 16 July 1899.
11 Quoted in A. Petersen, *Daniel De Leon – Pioneer Socialist Editor*, pp. 26–7. From a posthumous *People* editorial entitled 'At the Bier of "The Call"'.
12 Kuhn, 'Reminiscences', p. 29.
13 De Leon, Preface to *The Gold Sickle*, pp. iii–iv, 1 May 1904.
14 *Ibid.*, p. v.
15 A. Petersen, *Daniel De Leon – Orator*, p. 10.
16 R. Katz, 'With De Leon Since '89', p. 13.
17 The *People*, 19 August 1898.
18 *SLP Correspondence*, WSHS.
19 *Socialist Landmarks: Four Addresses*, p. 39.
20 *Daily People*, 20 July 1908.
21 *Socialist Landmarks*, pp. 51–3.

Chapter 3

1 K. Marx, *Selected Works* (Moscow, 1973), pp. 225–6.
2 De Leon, *Socialist Landmarks*, p. 85.
3 *Ibid*, p. 83.
4 *Ibid*, p. 90.
5 *Ibid*, p. 95.
6 *Ibid*, pp. 95–6.
7 *Ibid*, p. 97.
8 *Ibid*, p. 105.
9 *Ibid*, p. 118.
10 *Ibid*.
11 F. Lassalle, *Gesammelte Reden u. Lehriften*, III (Berlin, 1893), 5.58.
12 E. Browder, *Marx and America* (London, 1959), p. 47; see also p. 39.

13 C. Reeve, *The Life and Times of Daniel De Leon*, p. 150.
14 *Internationalism* (ICC) (Fall 1979); see also May–July 1980, no. 24.
15 Gompers, *Seventy Years of Life and Labor*, I, p. 385.
16 Kuhn, 'Reminiscences', p. 7.
17 *Ibid.*, pp. 7–8.
18 *Marx–Engels Selected Correspondence*, p. 169.
19 P. Z. Morgan to De Leon, 24 July 1896, in *SLP Correspondence*, WSHS.
20 Quoted in Dubofsky, *We Shall be All*, p. 65.
21 N. I. Stone, *The Attitude of the Socialist Towards The Trade Unions,* October 1899, p. 6.
22 'Preceding the ST & LA', the *People*, 19 July, 2 August, 16 August, 13 September 1986; reprinted from the original in *Daily People*, 1910.
23 *Ibid.*
24 Katz, 'With De Leon Since '89', p. 72.
25 O. Johnson, 'Daniel De Leon – Our Comrade', p. 120.
26 *Ibid.*, pp. 125–6; translated from the American-German by Clifford Slapper.
27 *The People*, 17 February 1895.
28 'A Debate on the Tactics of the ST & LA Toward Trade Unions Between Daniel De Leon and Job Harriman' (New York, 1900), p. 7.
29 *Ibid.*, p. 13 ff.; see Katz, 'With De Leon Since '89', pp. 78–81.
30 'A Debate on the Tactics of the ST & LA', p. 14.
31 *Ibid.*, p. 14.
32 *Ibid.*, p. 17.
33 *Proceedings of the First Convention of the IWW*, p. 151.
34 In fact, the IWW incorporated this slogan only into its 1908 Preamble, but it was, none the less, the policy of the Wobblies in 1905.

Chapter 4

1 See E. Hass, *The SLP and the Internationals*, p. 29.
2 'Trimming the Poodle', *Daily People*, 2 November 1908.
3 De Leon, *Socialist Landmarks*, p. 32.
4 De Leon, *Two Pages from Roman History*, p. 88.
5 'Trimming the Poodle'.
6 *Daily People*, 8 November 1913.
7 De·Leon, *A Socialist in Congress*, p. 9.
8 A. Bebel, *Women Under Socialism*, translator's preface, p. iv.
9 De Leon, *The Ballot and the Class Struggle*, p. 40.
10 I. Kipnis, *The American Socialist Movement, 1897–1912*, p. 278.
11 *Daily People*, 'Letter Box', 25 October 1903.
12 'A Word to the Proletariat of Spain', *Daily People*, 20 March 1898.
13 *Farmers' Alliance*, 7 May 1891, quoted in N. Pollack *The Populist Response to Industrial America*.

14 Pollack, *The Populist Response*, p. 95.
15 *Advocate* (Topeka, Kansas), 22 November 1893, cited in Pollack, *The Populist Respone*, p. 95.
16 De Leon, *Socialist Landmarks*, p. 56.
17 *Ibid.*, p. 59.
18 Cited by D. Herreshoff, *The Origins of American Marxism*, p. 119.
19 *The People*, 4 March 1895.
20 *SLP Correspondence*, WSHS.
21 Quoted in A. Petersen, *Bourgeois Socialism: Its Rise and Collapse in America – The Saga of the Reformist 'Socialist' Party* (NYLN, 1951), p. 31.
22 *Ibid.*, pp. 21-2.
23 De Leon, *Socialist Landmarks*, p. 63.
24 *Proceedings of Tenth SLP Convention*, p. 2.
25 *Ibid.*, p. 7.
26 *Ibid.*, p. 211.
27 Kuhn, 'Reminiscences', p. 28.
28 *Proceedings of Tenth SLP Convention*, Appendix, p. 254.
29 *Ibid.*, p. 86.
30 *Ibid.*, p. 93.
31 *Ibid.*, p. 101.
32 *Ibid.*, p. 102.
33 *Ibid.*, p. 93.
34 *Ibid.*, p. 76.
35 A. Petersen, *Daniel De Leon – Internationalist*, p. 16.
36 De Leon, *Flashlights of the Amsterdam Congress*, p. 20.
37 *Ibid.*, p. 192.
38 *Ibid.*, p. 149.
39 *Ibid.*, p. 9.
40 *Ibid.*, p. 13.
41 *Ibid.*, p. 34–5.
42 *Ibid.*, p. 37.
43 *Ibid.*, p. 47.
44 Hass, *The SLP and the Internationals*, p. 54.
45 *Ibid.*, p. 71.
46 De Leon, *A Socialist in Congress*, p. 29.
47 *Ibid.*, pp. 61–4.
48 O. Johnson, 'Daniel De Leon – Our Comrade', p. 93.
49 Katz, 'With De Leon', p. 89.

Chapter 5

1 De Leon, *Socialist Landmarks*, p. 162.
2 *Ibid.*, p. 148.

3 *Ibid.*, pp. 150, 159–60.
4 *Ibid.*, p. 157.
5 *Ibid.*, p. 158.
6 Katz, 'With De Leon', p. 108.
7 Quoted in M. Dubofsky, *'Big Bill' Haywood*, Appendix I, p. 158.
8 Kuhn, 'Reminiscences', p. 49.
9 *Proceedings of Tenth SLP Convention*, p. 237.
10 Connolly to Matheson, 30 January 1908.
11 *Proceedings of First Convention of the IWW*, p. 152.
12 Ibid., pp. 143–5.
13 Ibid., p. 147–51.
14 Quoted in A. Petersen's Preface to De Leon, *Socialist Landmarks*, 'Socialist Reconstruction', p. 180.
15 De Leon, *Socialist Landmarks*, p. 208.
16 *Ibid.*, p. 210.
17 *Ibid.*, p. 214.
18 *Ibid.*, p. 244.
19 *Ibid.*, p. 223 (emphasis in original).
20 *Ibid.*, p. 223.
21 *Ibid.*, p. 227.
22 *Ibid.*, p. 228.
23 *Ibid.*, p. 224.
24 Quoted in A. Lozovsky, *Marx and the Trade Unions*, p. 153, and De Leon's 'With Marx For Text', *Daily People*, 29 June 1907, in *Industrial Unionism – Selected Editorials by Daniel De Leon* (NYLN, 1931), p. 37.
25 De Leon, *Socialism versus Anarchism*, p. 27.
26 *Ibid.*, p. 28.
27 *Daily People*, 3 August 1909, in *Industrial Unionism – Selected Editorials by Daniel De Leon*, p. 43.
28 *Proceedings of the First Convention of the IWW*, p. 228.
29 *Ibid.*, p. 227.
30 De Leon, *Socialist Landmarks*, p. 229.
31 *Ibid.*, pp. 242–3.
32 De Leon, *As To Politics*, p. 46.
33 *Proceedings of the First Convention of the IWW*, p. 240.
34 C. Desmond Greaves, *The Life and Times of James Connolly*, p. 228.
35 De Leon, *As To Politics*, p. 69.
36 *Ibid.*, p. 78.
37 *Ibid.*, pp. 51–2.
38 *Ibid.*, p. 50.
39 De Leon, *Socialist Landmarks*, p. 57.
40 De Leon, *As To Politics*, p. 57.
41 *Ibid.*, p. 17.

42 *Ibid.*, p. 104.
43 De Leon, *Socialism versus Anarchism*, p. 35.
44 De Leon, *As To Politics*, p. 18.
45 *Ibid.*, p. 60.
46 The *People*, 16 October 1892.
47 De Leon, *As To Politics*, p. 61.
48 *Ibid.*, p. 61.
49 *Ibid.*, p. 112.
50 P. Brissenden, *The Industrial Workers of the World: A Study of American Syndicalism*, p. 141.
51 Quoted in De Leon, *Socialist Landmarks*, p. 181.
52 Brissenden, *Industrial Workers*, p. 239.
53 *Ibid.*, p. 178.
54 *Proceedings of Third IWW Convention*, p. 5.
55 *Industrial Union Bulletin*, 10 October 1908.

Chapter 6

1 S. Coleman, 'The Origin and Meaning of the Political Theory of Impossibilism', unpublished Ph.D thesis, University of London, 1984, Chapter 6.
2 T. A. Jackson, *Solo Trumpet* (London, 1953), p. 61.
3 Desmond Greaves, *James Connolly*, p. 149.
4 *Ibid.*, p. 148.
5 *Ibid.*, p. 150.
6 *Ibid.*, p. 150.
7 *Ibid.*, p. 150.
8 *O'Brien Papers*, NLI, n.d.
9 *Workers' Republic*, 3 October 1903.
10 Translator's Preface to Bebel, *Woman Under Socialism*, p. iii.
11 Marx, *Selected Works*, pp. 222–3.
12 *Weekly People*, 9 April 1904.
13 Preface to Bebel, *Woman Under Socialism*.
14 *Ibid.*, p. iv.
15 *Ibid.*, p. iv.
16 The *People*, 18 January 1902.
17 *Ibid.*
18 Desmond Greaves, *James Connolly*, p. 170.
19 The *People*, 28 May 1904, 18 June 1904.
20 *Ibid.*, 14 May 1904.
21 *Ibid.*, 11 June 1904.
22 *Ibid.*, 14 May 1904.
23 *Ibid.*, 7 May 1904.
24 *Ibid.*, 28 May 1904.

25 *Ibid.*, 14 May 1904.
26 *Ibid.*, 7 May 1904.
27 *O'Brien Papers*, NLI, 26 May 1904.
28 The *People*, 23 February 1907.
29 *Ibid.*, 2 March 1907.
30 *The Call* (New York), 24 November 1908.
31 *The Harp*, January 1908.
32 *Katz*, 'With De Leon', p. 126.
33 See De Leon, *The Vatican in Politics – Ultramontanism: The Roman Catholic Political Machine in Action*.

Chapter 7

1 *Daily People*, 13 August 1912.
2 *House of Representatatives*, 18 July 1912; quoted in Kuhn, 'Reminiscences', p. 70.
3 De Leon, *Socialism versus Individualism*, pp. 32–3.
4 Quoted in Petersen, *Bourgeois Socialism*, p. 202.
5 The *People*, 8 January 1893.
6 De Leon, 'Industrial Unionism' appendix to E. Hass, *Socialist Industrial Unionism* (NYLN, 1957), p. 55.
7 De Leon, Socialist Landmarks, p. 233.
8 *Ibid.*, p. 232.
9 *Ibid.*, p. 234.
10 Hass, *Socialist Industrial Unionism*, fold-out diagram between pp. 24 and 25.
11 A. Tomkins, *Socialism and Economic Power*, p. 10.
12 De Leon, *Socialist Landmarks*, p. 234.
13 De Leon, *Fifteen Questions About Socialism*, pp. 73–4.
14 *The Dawn*, 15 September 1889.
15 De Leon, *Fifteen Questions About Socialism*, p. 83.
16 *The Dawn*, 15 September 1889.
17 De Leon, *Fifteen Questions About Socialism*, p. 48.
18 *Ibid.*, pp. 18–232.
19 *Ibid.*, p. 13.
20 Bellamy, *Looking Backward*, p. 72.
21 S. Coleman, 'The economics of utopia: *Looking Backward* v. *News From Nowhere*', in *Journal of the William Morris Society*, (Spring 1989).
22 De Leon, *Capitalism versus Socialism*, p. 50.
23 The People, 6 December 1896; *Proceedings of the Tenth Convention of the SLP*, p. 7; see discussion of this in Chapter 2.
24 The *People*, 21 February 1904.
25 De Leon, *Socialism versus Individualism*, p. 45.

Chapter 8

1 Quoted in Kuhn, 'Reminiscences', pp. 59–61.
2 De Leon, *Unity*, (NYLN, 1908), pp. 9–11.
3 See E. Debs, 'A Plea for Solidarity' in J. M. Bernstein (ed.), *Writings and Speeches of Eugene V. Debs* (1948), pp. 370–3.
4 *Daily People*, 16 July 1908.
5 *Ibid.*, 3 October 1911.
6 Johnson, 'De Leon – Our Comrade', p. 101.
7 Quoted in Peterson, *De Leon – From Reform to Revolution*, p. 41.
8 De Leon, 'Reform or Revolution', pp. 61–3.
9 De Leon, *Two Pages from Roman History*, p. 69.
10 *Proceedings of the Tenth SLP Convention*, Appendix, p. 256.
11 De Leon, *Marxian Science and the Colleges*, p. 19.
12 *Ibid.*, p. 20.
13 *Daily People*, 14 February 1913.
14 *Daily People*, 14 February 1913.
15 De Leon, *As To Politics*, pp. 107–8.
16 *Weekly People*, 16 May 1914.
17 Quoted in Petersen, *De Leon – Pioneer Socialist Editor*, pp. 38–9.
18 21 May 1914; quoted in A. Petersen, *Daniel De Leon, Social Architect*, I, (NYLN, 1941), p. 288.
19 *Appeal to Reason*, 12 April 1912, quoted in Petersen, *Bourgeois Socialism*, p. 154–5.
20 *National Ripsaw*, 8 (5); quoted in Petersen, *Bourgeois Socialism*, p. 155.
21 *Daily People*, 5 January 1914.
22 J. Schlossberg, *The Workers and their World* (New York 1935), p. 340.
23 See the *Western Socialist*, 33 (252), 1966, for a historical account of this tradition.
24 *Socialist Standard*, December 1905.
25 The *Socialist*, February 1904.
26 *Industrial Unionist*, March 1908.
27 The *Socialist*, January 1913, quoted in R. Challinor, *The Origins of British Bolshevism*, p. 98.
28 See Report in the *Edinburgh Evening News*, 23 August 1904.
29 For accounts, see the *Socialist*, December 1904; and F. Budgen, *Myselves When Young* (Oxford, 1970), p. 86.
30 G. Aldred, *Pioneers of Anti-Parliamentarism* (Glasgow, 1940), p. 74.
31 A. Bevan, *In Place Of Fear* (London, 1952), p. 38.
32 E. Heffer, 'The case for industrial unionism', in *A Socialist Review* (1958).
33 A. Petersen, 'Daniel De Leon – Social Architect', quoted in Petersen, *Karl Marx and Marxian Science*, p. 185.
34 A. Petersen, *Proletarian Democracy versus Dictatorships and Despotism* (NYLN, 1932), p. 12.

35 V. I. Lenin, *Collected Works*, 26, p. 175.

36 *Ibid.*, 36, p. 528.

37 *Ibid.*, 31, p. 53.

38 L. G. Raisky, *Daniel De Leon: The Struggle Against Opportunism in the American Labor Movement* (NYLN, 1932), pp. 85–6.

39 De Leon, *Two Pages from Roman History*, p. 93.

40 De Leon, *Socialism versus Anarchism*, p. 28.

41 De Leon, *Socialist Landmarks*, p. 60.

41 *Proceedings of the Second Convention of the IWW*.

42 *Ibid.*

43 Quoted in Petersen, *Bourgeois Socialism*, p. 46 (my emphasis).

45 *Disruption and Disrupters* (SLP, 1935), pp. 4–5.

46 E. Hass, 'Why I Resigned from the SLP', in *Socialit Forum* (July 1969).

47 *The SLP and the USSR* (NYLN), 1978).

48 I. Stone, *Adversary in the House* (New York, 1949), pp. 312–13.

49 De Leon, *Socialism versus Anarchism*, p. 36.

Suggested reading and bibliography

De Leon's works are published in pamphlet form and make for simple and lively reading, especially when the reader understands that they were not composed as literature but are transcribed speeches or collected newspaper articles. The best introductory work to read is *Socialist Landmarks*, which contains four of De Leon's most popular and effective addresses: 'What Means This Strike?' provides a particularly good starting point.

Books about De Leon have tended to be quite unsatisfactory. Reeve's *The Life and Times of Daniel De Leon* (1972) contains some useful biographical material, especially in the introduction by Oakley C. Johnson, which was written on the basis of information provided by De Leon's son, Solon. Reeve's biography attempts to fit De Leon's ideas into the conception of American labour history adopted by the Communist Party of the United States, and such a perspective is too narrow to explain the broader political themes which underlay De Leon's thinking. Seretan's biography *Daniel De Leon: The Odyssey of an American Marxist* (1979) falls into the trap of investigating the caricature of De Leon as a psychopolitical character; the same approach is adopted by several other books listed here which deal with or mention De Leon, and, as I explained in the Preface to this book, I regard such an approach as entirely pointless. Petersen's writings on De Leon contain much that is of biographical value, but the writer's strenuous efforts to deify his subject renders much of his material ridiculous. The best published work on De Leon is by Herreshoff, whose book raises many perceptive and stimulating points; the same author has a chapter on De Leon in Goldberg's book, *American Radicals: Some Problems and Perspectives* (1957). The unpublished doctoral thesis by Stevenson is the best scholarly work on the subject of De Leon: it is very carefully researched, using the De Leon papers kept at the Wisconsin State Historical Society (WSHS) in Madison, Wisconsin. The particular value of Stevenson's work is that he connects De Leon's socialist perspectives with those of other Marxists in Europe at the same time.

Little material has been published on the Socialist Labor Party (SLP). Bell, Foner and Quint provide limited material on the party, as does Hillquit, although the latter's role in the SLP split of 1899 must be understood in assessing his book historiographically. A forthcoming history of the SLP by ex-SLP members Frank Girard and Ben Perry should cover the subject well.

These two writers have covered SLP history in some detail in the *Discussion Bulletin* which is edited by Girard and obtainable from P.O. Box 1564, Grand Rapids, MI 49501, USA. The SLP still publishes the *People* (fortnightly) and it, together with other SLP publications, are available from P.O. Box 50218, Palo Alto, CA 94303, USA. Other De Leonist publications are the *Socialist Republic*, available from the Industrial Union Party, P.O. Box 80, New York, NY 10159, USA; and the *De Leonist Society Bulletin*, which is available from P.O. Box 22055, San Francisco, CA 94122, USA.

The books in the following list all contain references to De Leon or his ideas, or else (as in the case of Beer) provide interesting background material on the period. Dates of pamphlets published by NYLN refer to original publication, but where I have used a reprinted copy in the text I have given the date for that as well. Some De Leon pamphlets have changed title as they were reprinted but the texts have not been altered.

Bebel, A., *Woman Under Socialism* (NYLN), 1904).

Beer, T., *The Mauve Decade* (New York 1926).

Bell, D., *Marxian Socialism in the United States* (Princeton, 1967).

Bellamy, E., *Looking Backwards* (Harmondsworth, 1986).

Berrisford, Ellis, P., *James Connolly: Selected Writings* (Harmondsworth, 1973.) pp. 147–87.

Brissendon, P., *The Industrial Workers of the World: A Study of American Syndicalism* (New York 1919).

Brommel, B., *Eugene V. Debs: Spokesman for Labor and Socialism* (Chicago 1978).

Browder, E., *Marx and America* (London, 1959).

Challinor, R., *The Origins of British Bolshevism* (London 1977).

Chamberlin, J. *Farewell to Reform* (New York, 1932), see pp. 81–5.

Chewter, D. M., 'The History of the Socialist Labour Party of Great Britain from 1902–21, with Specail Reference to the Development of its Ideas', unpublished B. Litt. thesis, Oxford 1965.

Cork Workers' Club, *The Connolly–De Leon Controversy On Wages, Marriage and the Church* (Cork, 1986).

De Leon, D., *Socialism versus Anarchism* (NYLN, 1901–1970).

——, *Two Pages from Roman History* (NYLN), 1903–1915.

——, *As To Politics* (NYLN, 1907–1966.

——, Unity: An Address Delivered by Daniel De Leon at New Pythagoras Hall, New York, 21 February 1908 (NYLN, 1908).

——, *The Ballot and the Class Struggle* (NYLN, 1909, 1971.

——, *A Socialist in Congress*, (NYLN, 1912, 1962).

——, *Fifteen Questions About Socialism*, (NYLN, 1914, 1967).

——, *Capitalism versus Socialism* (NYLN, 1915, 1969).

——, *Evolution of a Liberal: From Reform to Reaction* (NYLN, 1926, 1965).

Suggested reading and bibliography

———, *The Vatican in Politics – Ultramontanism: The Roman Catholic Political Machine in Action* (NYLN, 1928, 1962).

———, *Flashlights of the Amsterdam Congress* (NYLN, 1929).

———, *Industrial Unionism: Selected Editorials by Daniel De Leon* (NYLN, 1931).

———, *Marxian Science and the Colleges* (NYLN, 1932, 1966).

———, *Socialism versus Individualism* (NYLN, 1942, 1966).

———, *Socialist Landmarks*, (1952, 1957), includes 'Reform or Revolution', 'What Means This Strike?' 'The Burning Question of Trades Unionism' and 'Socialist Reconstruction of Society'.

Desmond Greaves, C., *The Life and Times of James Connolly* (London, 1972).

Draper, T., *The Roots of American Communism*, (New York 1957)

Dubofsky, M., *We Shall Be All: A History of the IWW* (New York 1969).

———, *'Big Bill' Haywood* (Manchester, 1987).

Emmett, W. H.,. *The Marxian Economic Handbook* (London, 1925), Appendix C.

Fitz, D., 'Was Daniel De Leon a Reformist?', *Workers' Democracy*, 24 (Summer 1987).

Foner, S., *Jack London* (New York, 1958) pp. 64–5.

George, H., *Progress and Poverty* (New York, 1879).

Ghent, W. J., 'De Leon', in *Dictionary of National Biography* V, pp. 222–4.

Goldberg, H., *American Radicals: Some Problems and Perspectives* (New York, 1957).

Hass, E., *The SLP and the Internationals* (NYLN, 1949).

———, *Socialist Industrial Unonism* (NYLN, 1940, 1957).

Haywood, W., *Bill Haywood's Book: Autobiography of William D. Haywood* (New York, 1929).

Herreshoff, D., *The Orgins of American Marxism: From the Transcendentalists to De Leon* (New York: 1973).

Hillquit, M., *History of Socialism in the United States* (New York 1903).

———, *Loose Leaves from a Busy Life* (New York, 1934).

Holbrook, S., H., *Dreamers of the American Dream* (New York 1957).

Internationalism, 'Debate re De Leon between *Internationalism* and *New Socialist, Internationalism*, 24, pp. 11–22.

Jackson, T. A., *Solo Trumpet* (London, 1953).

Johnson, O., *Daniel De Leon* (NYLN, 1923).

———, 'Daniel De Leon – Our Comrade' in *Daniel De Leon: The Man and His Work* (NYLN, 1919, 1969).

Katz, R., 'With De Leon Since '89', in *Daniel De Leon: The Man and His Work* (NYLN, 1919, 1969).

Kipnis, I., *The American Socialist Movement*, 1897–1912 (New York, 1952).

Kuhn, H., 'Reminiscences of Daniel De Leon', in *Daniel De Leon: The Man and His Work* (NYLN, 1919, 1969).

Laslett, J. H. M., 'Socialism and the American Federation of Labor', unpublished D.Phil. thesis, Oxford, 1962.

Lozovsky, A., *Marx and the Trade Unions* (New York, 1935).

McKee, D., 'The Intellectual and Historical Influences Shaping the Political Theory of Daniel De Leon', unpublished Ph.D. thesis, Columbia, 1953.

Obermann, K., *Joseph Weydemeyer: Pioneer of American Socialism* (New York, 1947).

Petersen, A., *Proletarian Democracy versus Dictatorship and Despotism* (NYLN, 1932).

———, *Daniel De Leon: From Reform to Revolution, 1886–1936* (NYLN, 1937).

———, *Daniel De Leon – Pioneer Socialist Editor* (NYLN, 1937).

———, *Daniel De Leon – The Uncompromising* (NYLN, 1939).

———, *Daniel De Leon – Socialist Architect* (NYLN, 1941).

———, *Daniel De Leon – Orator* (NYLN, 1942).

———, *Karl Marx and Marxian Science* (NYLN, 1943).

———, *Daniel De Leon – Social Scientist* (NYLN, 1945).

———, *Revolutionary Milestones* (NYLN, 1946).

———, *Daniel De Leon – Internationalist* (NYLN, 1948).

———, *Reviling the Great* (NYLN, 1949), pp. 62–88.

———, *Bourgeois Socialism: Its Rise and Collapse in America – The Saga of the Reformist 'Socialist' Party* (NYLN, 1951), p. 31.

———, *De Leonist Milestones* (NYLN, 1952).

Pollock, N., *The Populist Response to Industrial America* (New York, 1962).

Quint, H., *The Forging of American Socialism: Origins of the Modern Movement* (Columbia, 1953).

Raisky, L. G., *Daniel De Leon: the Struggle Against Opportunism in the American Labor Movement* (NYLN, 1932).

Reeve, C., *The Life and Times of Daniel De Leon* (New York, 1972).

Rubel, M., and Crump, J., *Non-Market Socialism in the Nineteenth and Twentieth Centuries* (London, 1987).

Schlossberg, J., *The Workers and their World* (New York, 1935).

Seretan, L. G., *Daniel De Leon: the Odyssey of an American Marxist* (Harvard, 1979).

Socialist Labor Party, *Proceedings of the Ninth Convention of the Socialist Labor Party* (New York, 1897).

———, *Proceedings of the Tenth Convention of the Socialist Labor Party* (New York, 1901).

———, *Socialist Labor Party, 1890–1930* (NYLN, 1931).

———, *Golden Jubilee of De Leonism* (NYLN, 1940).

Stalvey, J. B., 'Daniel De Leon: A Study of Marxian Orthodoxy in the United States', unpublished Ph.D. thesis, University of Illinois, 1947.

Stevenson, J. A., 'Daniel De Leon: The Relationship of the Socialist Labor Party and European Marxism, 1890–1914', unpublished Ph.D. thesis, University of Wisconsin, 1977.

Stone, N. I., *The Attitude of the Socialists Towards the Trade Unions* (New York, 1899).

Tomkins, A., *Socialism and Economic Power* (British SLP, 1965).

Tuchman, B., *The Proud Tower* (New York, 1966).

Wolfe, B. D., *Marx and America* (New York, 1934).

Index